YOU DON'T NEED

FOLLOWERS

TO BE A

LEADER

*Embracing the Spirit of Leadership
In the Age of Influence and Narcissism*

SEBASTIEN RICHARD

You Don't Need Followers to Be a Leader: Embracing the Spirit of Leadership in the Age of Influence and Narcissism

DISCLAIMER

The author and publisher specifically disclaim all responsibility for any liability, loss or risk, personal or otherwise, that is incurred as a consequence, directly or indirectly, of the use and application of any of the contents of this book.

The inclusion of masculine or feminine genders or titles in this book is intended to encompass both genders and should not be interpreted as a leadership limitation based on gender.

This publication is meant as a source of valuable information for the reader, however, it is not meant as a substitute for direct expert assistance when needed—medical or otherwise. If such a level of assistance is required, the services of a competent professional should be sought.

This book may also contain images, quotes, and portions of text that have been included under the doctrine of fair use. These materials are utilized for purposes such as commentary, criticism, education, and research. The inclusion of such content is intended to enhance the reader's understanding and engagement with the subject matter. The use of these materials is in good faith and aligns with the principles of fair use as defined in copyright law.

To my beloved wife, my bride and joy:

Elisabeth

TABLE OF CONTENTS

"I returned and saw under the sun that…

The race is not to the swift,
Nor the battle to the strong,
Nor bread to the wise,
Nor riches to men of understanding,
Nor favor to men of skill;
But time and chance happen to them all."

~Ecclesiastes 9:11

King Solomon, circa 935 BC

ACKNOWLEDGEMENTS

To all the leaders who have been guides and mentors throughout the various seasons of my life, too many to name comprehensively, *thank you.*

To all the pastors, teachers, and researchers, whether in person or online, who have brought their knowledge and wisdom to the forefront through platforms such as YouTube and Facebook for others to glean from, *thank you.*

In my writing classes and while tutoring authors, I often emphasize the profound connection between being a nonfiction author and assuming a leadership role. *"As an author,"* I often explain, *"You have a distinct power. You wield the power to share knowledge, offer guidance, influence, encourage, and bless others—a role embedded in the very word "authority," from which the word "author" is derived."*

And so, it is with this in mind that I wish to thank all the leaders who ventured to write books that exhort us to a life well lived. *Thank you!*

My journey through countless books has been enriched by the wisdom and teachings of numerous instructors, wise men, and leaders. Each has served as a mentor, contributing uniquely to my growth, whether personal or spiritual. As philosopher René Descartes aptly noted, *"The reading of all good books is like a conversation with the finest minds of past centuries."*

I also want to express my gratitude to my beloved wife, Elisabeth, whose insightful perspectives and keen observations on leadership in the era of social media have played a significant role in shaping the content of this book. Liz, my love, I am grateful for the countless hours we have spent delving into these meaningful conversations. Your astute understanding has been indispensable in shaping this literary work.

I also wish to extend my deepest gratitude to the John Maxwell Team Faculty. My appreciation goes to the late Ed DeCosta, as well as Paul Martinelli and to John C. Maxwell himself—not just for teaching and showing the way, but also for instilling in me invaluable JMT DNA (John Maxwell Team DNA). This DNA emphasizes the prioritization of others' needs and interests over one's own. For this crucial life principle, and so many others you teach, John, *thank you.*

A heartfelt tribute is dedicated to the late Dr. Myles Munroe. Your teachings acted as a corrective lens during a critical juncture in my life's journey. Without your unique insights, I might have succumbed to despair and abandoned my pursuit of making a meaningful impact in this world.

Finally, I wish to express my gratitude to all those who, through their examples of both good and bad leadership, have illuminated the path, showing me what to emulate and what to avoid as a leader.

Thank you all for being integral to my leadership journey.

Sincerely,

Sebastien Richard

PREFACE

In today's high stakes world where performance in all spheres is measured mostly by results and numbers, many find themselves wanting. Leaders are no exception.

For many would-be leaders and existing leaders, the scale of their leadership ability is measured by the number of their followers. Whether on YouTube, Instagram, X, or TikTok, or as reflected by their sales, the more followers they have, the better they are rated as leaders. But is this measuring stick reflective of their true worth as leaders?

The purpose of this book is to serve as a tribute and a roadmap to individuals who dedicate themselves to adding value to others and who relentlessly push forward in a world that often fails to appreciate their true significance—their strength of purpose, determination, imagination, creativity, resilience, and unwavering resolve against all odds.

The content found within its pages will encourage and appeal to:

- ✓ Business owners… *without clients.*
- ✓ Network Marketers… *without a team.*
- ✓ Thought leaders… *without thinkers.*
- ✓ Podcasters… *without listeners.*
- ✓ Authors… *without readers.*
- ✓ Entrepreneurs… *without sales.*
- ✓ Preachers… *without converts.*
- ✓ Teachers… *without students.*
- ✓ Artists… *without recognition.*

- ✓ Speakers… *without an audience.*
- ✓ Coaches… *without clients.*
- ✓ Dreamers… *without opportunities.*
- ✓ Legacy builders… *without an heir.* And, of course, in a more generalized sense…
- ✓ Leaders… *without followers.*

It is with you in mind, *dear leaders without followers*, that I wrote this book. The following pages offer not only value, affirmation, and encouragement, but also insight and a renewed sense of worth, direction, and purpose.

I sincerely hope the reading of this book will deliver you from:

- Low self-esteem.
- False expectations.
- Feeling like a failure.
- Seeking approval.
- And most of all… I hope it will deliver you from *seeking followers to feel validated.*

Trust that you are worthy of being called leaders. Because, ultimately, when everything is said and done…

You don't need followers to be a leader!

INTRODUCTION

Writing this book has proven much harder than I initially thought. Much, much harder. It all began with a simple idea–a concept, really. When I finally realized that my own results (followers, recognition, book sales, and/or customers) didn't reflect my outer abilities, knowledge, inner fortitude, effort, human worth, and value as a thought-leader; that's when it dawned on me that I probably wasn't the only one. Hence, my original goal was to create a brief booklet that would teach and empower individuals to stay positive and motivated despite setbacks and/or a reduced number of followers. I told Elisabeth (my wife) that it probably wouldn't exceed 20 pages. I also told her it would take me a week to write.

I was wrong on both counts, obviously.

Not only did it require far more than 20 pages to complete, but it also took a much bigger effort, and much more time than anticipated to write. It took me well over five years to research, collect the facts, develop the insight, and summon the bravery necessary to write and publish this work.

Courage, you ask? Yes, *courage*. The truth is that tackling a subject this controversial and counter-intuitive is *not* something I took to lightly. Not only does teaching people they can be leaders without followers is hard, but it also flies in the face of the best and most popular leadership concepts that are in vogue right now. Even more so; it contradicts well-established leadership studies and the most revered leadership teachers out there. And that, in all honesty, scared me. After all, discussing the notion of true leaders without followers is a lot like talking about *weak lions* or *dry water*. People look at you like you've lost your mind, like there is no such thing. The majority of people believe such an animal does not exist. However, the evidence surrounding us confirms the existence of this peculiar creature.

As an author, I usually don't shy away from tackling difficult or even controversial subjects. But writing a book about how *you can be a leader without any followers* can really get you the wrong kind of attention. In the worse case scenario, if I fail to present this case properly, I could go down in history as a deluded fool. But despite this gloomy contemplation, I decided to take the leap.

So, dear reader, as you hold this book, I am here with you, ready to embark on this journey. I am ready to get you into my world and my thoughts. And you, it seems, are ready to benefit from my musings, findings, and theses.

So, go ahead, don't let anything stop you.

My Leadership Journey

I cannot tackle this subject without first being very candid and open with you, dear reader.

When I began my leadership training with *The John Maxwell Team*, back in 2016, I was very excited. I really liked the principles taught by the organization, and mostly by Dr. John C. Maxwell—who is arguably the most renowned leadership teacher of all-time. The curriculum, faculty, and content offered is simply *world class*. I devoured it.

Now, I knew I wasn't green when it came to the subject of leadership; thanks to my many years of Church ministry, reading, thinking, and studying many lanes of knowledge, including leadership and personal growth. In fact, I already considered myself a potent leader in some ways; a diamond in the rough, if you will. Back in the day, elders and leaders in my Church validated this for me. But on the flip side, I also knew *I had a lot to learn.*

At the leadership conferences I attended or watched online, high-profile speakers often repeated a saying based on an old African (some say Chinese) proverb. The saying was:

"He who thinks he is leading,
and has no one following, is only taking a walk."

The first time I heard it, not only did it make me chuckle, but I agreed with it wholeheartedly. I mean, like, 'duh!' it's obvious—right? Leaders *lead people.* So, we judge accordingly. The math is simple enough. Good leaders have followers, right? And, chances are, the more followers, the better the leader. *Right?*

And so it was that I believed in this leadership proverb for a long time.

As I embarked on my personal growth journey, I discovered my purpose as a writer, teacher, and entrepreneur, shaping a compelling vision for my future. I finally knew where I wanted to go and what I wanted to be in life. So, along with Elisabeth (who is also a John Maxwell Team certified leadership coach) I founded a faith-based leadership training organization: *Thriving on Purpose* (thrivingonpurpose.com).

I thus initiated a search for speaking engagements in my vicinity and started offering my services. Inspired by John C. Maxwell, my desire was (and still is) to empower others through my words and teachings, encouraging them to become the best version of themselves. My mindset was quite strong and I couldn't be deterred in my endeavors.

In 2017, on fire and feeling unstoppable, I wrote my first leadership book, which was published as *Lead Like a Superhero*. In it, I distilled most of what I knew about impactful leadership. I was even able to get one of the most sought-after motivational speakers in the world (at the time) to endorse it: Mel Robbins. I was convinced that this book would be the key to reaching greater levels of success.

For one of the first times in my life, my mindset was aligning with my natural talents and abilities (teaching, writing, speaking). I worked hard; I believed in myself, and I believed the only limits were in my mind.

- I knew I possessed leadership qualities.

- I understood and embraced my God-given purpose.
- My wife thought of me as a good husband and leader for our family.
- People at my church perceived me as a leader.
- I had a plan and a vision for what I wanted to accomplish.

Things looked on the up and up. Nevertheless, after two more years of hustling, bustling, and grinding, I noticed something was missing. Something I thought crucial.

When I looked over my shoulder, I noticed I had *no followers*. None, zero, nada, zilch.

Truth be told, after every speaking engagement, nobody came to see me for more. Despite advertising my book and promoting our services, no one showed interest in coaching, speaking, or leadership trainings. And while I may not be as skilled as Tony Robbins, I am a pretty good speaker. Even with live teaching videos, blogs, and thought-provoking memes on social media, the engagement was disappointing.

Moreover, Lead Like a Superhero had been released for over 2 years by then. The sales were, um, well, you know… let's just say I hadn't made it to the New York Times bestseller list yet.

Elisabeth and I had invested *tens of thousands of dollars and tens of thousands of hours* to further our own personal growth, knowledge, and competence. We had even re-mortgaged our house!

We invested in books, courses, online academies, daily podcasts, motivational videos, entrepreneurial seminars, and more! We used credit cards to pay for all the monthly dues along the way to keep our advertising and website going. In addition to publishing more books, I also started a podcast called *The Thriving on Purpose Podcast*, which focuses on faith, leadership, and personal growth. We had a YouTube channel where we posted our podcast teachings and other videos. We believed this was a short-term investment that would soon pay off.

We were wrong.

At some point, after months and years of this, I had to take a long, hard, and honest look at myself. When the results were still slim to none, I began thinking that I had *misled* myself (pun intended) into believing I was a leader. I engaged in deep self-reflection and evaluated my situation. I thought, *"Is it possible that I completely deluded myself into believing I am a leader? Did my reality check just bounce? Did I just pull the leadership equivalent of a bad audition on American Idol?"*

The old African proverb kept replaying in my mind, repeating itself endlessly, pointing an accusing finger.

For all intents and purposes, it now seemed obvious that *I was only taking a walk.*

My Epiphany

But then, after some months of disenchantment, *something extraordinary happened.* A shift took place on my leadership journey—a God-sent epiphany that would forever alter my self-perception.

Before I proceed, I must confess that I've always had reservations about the idea of having just one teacher. Being naturally curious, I've always sought diverse perspectives and teachings from experts, teachers, or gurus in any field. Leadership was no exception.

So, in the course of my leadership journey, I sought to acquire knowledge from a wide range of sources, even those that presented unconventional or controversial ideas. Doing so led me to many great thoughts and teachings on leadership that I otherwise never would have found if I weren't curious by nature.

So, one day, I found on YouTube a leadership training series taught by the late Dr. Myles Munroe titled: *Leading Edge Leadership.*

In this teaching series, Dr. Munroe said the following jaw-dropping statement:

"You were created to lead, but not to lead people. This is a difficult concept, but I teach it all over the world. Your culture tells you that to be a leader, you need followers.

I disagree.

Now, don't get me wrong; I used to believe that. I was taught the old proverb: 'He who thinketh he leadeth and hath no one following, is only taking a walk.' I used to believe that, but not anymore.

First of all, I don't believe you need followers to be a leader. All great and true leaders in history never sought followers. When a person seeks followers, that is proof to me that they are not leaders. They have ego problems. They have self-concept problems. They have self-esteem problems. They need other people to give them value. This is not leadership; this is a disease. It is called low self-worth. And there are many of them in our nations… with titles!"

After hearing these atoning words, I felt like a *truth lightning* hit me! It was as if God spoke to me directly, addressing something I desperately needed to understand.

Dr. Munroe's teachings on leadership completely shifted my perspective on the nature of leadership. It changed my life. It made me understand and appropriate that followers do not determine a leader's ability of worth. It made me appreciate my own journey better. I must say, it had a profound impact on my development as a leader and allowed me to move beyond the cultural fixation on gaining followers for validation.

Only Taking a Walk?

I love going for walks, particularly on brisk mornings in spring or summer. I live out in the country where the air is crisp at dawn. I love filling my lungs with the fresh air, listening to the chirping of the birds, and watching the rays of the sun as they peer through the forest branches. I also like greeting the cows and horses by the side of the road as I pass them by. Taking walks is, for me, therapeutic. It's not about the destination, it's about the journey, right? This, in itself, made me re-think the tirade about *'only taking a walk.'*

When we consider the old African proverb at face value, we neglect a couple of important details.

Yes, the avatar in question is, according to the saying, not leading. Although he may think he is leading, he is *'just taking a walk'*. But this begs three very important, albeit highly hypothetical, questions:

- Why is he taking a walk?
- Where is he going? *And most important…*
- What makes him think he is leading?

Please bear with me for a moment as we go down this rabbit trail.

As J. R. R. Tolkien once put it, *"not all who wander are lost."* We know that leaders are momentum makers, right? Hence, where there is no movement, we could assume there is no leadership. Period. So, the fact that this fictional person is *walking* means he is not idle. He's moving forward. It's a good start. Nobody follows idle people. The Scripture says, in 2 Corinthians 5:7, *"for we walk by faith, not by sight."*

So, at least, he's got this: he's advancing, moving forward. Good. It's a start.

But *where is he going?*

Ah! Now, that is a very crucial question. You see, the direction someone is going can enthrall potential followers or deter them. No matter how powerful your vision; if where you are going is risky, difficult, costly, or an uncharted territory, gaining followers will make it so much more difficult.

For example, many individuals would willingly follow someone sponsoring a trip to Disney World. On the contrary, *few* might be inclined to follow a leader on a self-funded missionary trip to a third-world country, where personal risks, including potential loss of life, are involved. Even if the person leading the missionary journey is highly skilled, they may still have fewer followers than a less competent leader who is giving away a trip to Disneyland. Consequently, the number of followers a leader attracts is heavily influenced by their chosen destination.

Another point to consider is, *what makes him think he is leading?*

There are two potential answers here. The most obvious is the one that the proverb alludes to: he isn't leading at all. He is delusional. He thinks of himself too highly. His reality check bounced. In that sense, the proverb is spot on.

On the other hand, what if he is in fact leading... but without any followers? What if he is onto something that nobody has seen yet? He might be a revolutionary. A trailbreaker. He might have a special calling. Perhaps he belongs to that small group of individuals in history who were ahead of their time as leaders, but didn't have any followers (at least initially). He could be one of those leaders who has difficulty connecting with people, which has led to a lack of followers despite his vision and calling. Some authentic leaders from the past have also encountered this scenario. I will expound more on those in the course of this book.

So, maybe you're like I was. Maybe you have been told that you are *only taking a walk*. Maybe you have lost your confidence and vision as a result. Rest assured, there is hope. Don't lose hope; try to enjoy your walk in the meantime.

Why Do Some Fake It?

In today's world, where everything moves quickly and success is emphasized, it's easy to feel down on ourselves when our hard work doesn't yield any results. That's the reason why many people begin as posers. They are convinced that adopting the *'Fake it 'Till You Make It'* philosophy is the key to attaining quicker results, social proof, or recognition. Consequently, they resort to manipulating their numbers, outcomes, and persona. In order to influence people and build a community, they invent stories of achievement. Bottom line, they talk *as though* they have those coveted results, when in fact, they have no success or following to speak of. At the end of the day, no matter how we try to disguise it, faking it is synonymous with lying.

Dr. S.I. McMillen, in his book *None of These Diseases*, tells the following story:

A young woman wanted to go to college, but her heart sank when she read the question on the application blank that asked, "Are you a leader?" Being both honest and conscientious, she wrote, "No," and returned the application, expecting the worst.

To her surprise, she received this letter from the college: "Dear applicant: A study of the application forms reveals that this year our college will have 1452 new leaders. We are accepting you because we feel that it is imperative that they have at least one follower."

As the above story shows, most people *'fake it 'till they make it'* because they are insecure. It's understandable to feel frustrated when you have the potential to influence but don't have any followers. It really makes you question yourself. Once you have been to the arena and all you heard were crickets, is it time to pack your bags? That's the specific pain point I address in this instance. It is a very silent pain-point that rarely, if ever, goes addressed because of the stigma associated with it. In fact, it is actually passed the point of pain. It's something worse.

In today's society, the absence of followers on platforms like Twitter, Instagram, or Facebook can cause leaders and aspiring leaders to feel… ashamed.

So, in a very real sense, it's not a *pain-point* anymore… it's a *shame-point*.

And those who become ashamed because of a lack of followers are, in a way, victims of a stigma. Even the strongest leader, if he has no followers, might fall for this trap. And yes, that's all it is: *a mindset trap*.

On the next pages, you'll acquire strategies to overcome this psychological shame-point. By the book's end, I hope you'll have conquered the urge to "fake it till you make it." In fact, I believe the genuineness and transparency shared here will encourage you to *face it till you make it*. The insights shared within these pages will hearten you to get up, work hard; and if you fail, stand back up and face it again. And if you fail again? Simple. Get back up and repeat the process.

Dustin McKissen, in an article for *Inc.com* titled *Why Being a Leader Can Mean Going It Alone*, wrote the following:

"Here are two truths:

1- *Real leaders don't wait until someone is standing behind them before they take a bold step forward.*

2- *There is no cheaper or meaningless word in today's world than "follower."*

If all it takes to be a leader is to have followers, then anyone with a X (Twitter) handle is a leader."

Dear reader, you likely picked up this book because its subject matter strikes a chord with you. For all I know, you may be *going it alone* right now. I dare venture to say that if you picked up this book, you might be *a leader without followers*—for now, anyway.

No worries. If that's the case, you'll be happy to read in the following pages that you are, in fact, not alone. You'll find out that, while you may not have any followers, you're in pretty good company. You will also discover that followers do not make the leader.

I hope that after finishing this book, you will be motivated to begin or continue building your vision, no matter the challenges. I hope that my words will encourage you to stay motivated and not let the number of followers discourage you ever again. Likewise, and conversely, it is also my hope that you will not get puffed up with a false sense of pride if you have hordes of screaming fans behind you. This book, if I've done my job correctly, will assure you of your *personal leadership*. When you're done consuming it, you'll grasp that you are a leader, irrespective of having followers.

And so, *You Don't Need Followers to Be a Leader* serves as an offering to those who have the backbone to lead their own lives, confront their status quo, discover, develop, and share their gifts, push through adversity, follow their dreams, get back up after they fail and fall. To those who believe God for the impossible, rely on His grace and favor, and who, in the end, don't care who takes notice.

CHAPTER 1

The Spirit of Leadership

"True leadership is an attitude that naturally inspires and motivates others, and it comes from an internalized discovery about yourself."

~Myles Munroe

Before we attempt any kind of explanation on how one can be a leader without followers, we must first understand what leadership entails. We must redefine what it means to be a leader. We must clarify, re-define, and deconstruct, if that's at all possible, what leadership truly is. Indeed, the term "leadership" has been misused, misunderstood, poorly defined, categorized, and thus made to seem unattainable.

True leadership is not a position, achievement, or even a recognition; *it is a process*. The process of leadership begins with self-discovery, followed by others discovering and following you.

In order to be a leader, we must lead our own lives (more on this later); and this means that we must know ourselves, know our purpose, and channel our gifts into fruition in order to *serve* others.

God gave each and every one of us gifts, talents, and abilities. We cannot possibly lead if we do not serve these gifts to others. In essence, leadership is very aptly defined by this quote of Dr. Myles Munroe:

"Every human being was created to dominate and lead in an area of gifting." ~Myles Munroe

As I mentioned when quoting Dr. Munroe in the book's Introduction, most individual's purpose is not to be leaders of people. This statement in the realm of leadership studies was one of the most revelatory (and shocking) I had ever come across. It is barely, if ever, opined or much less discussed. And yet, upon close study, observation, scrutiny, and experience of what this entails, I now fully agree with that notion. The more I elaborate, the more I think you will agree as well.

Understand this: we were created to be leaders of our gift (particular talent, ability) by discovering it, developing it, and serving it to as many people as possible. If we present our gift to others with class, quality, and quantity, we are in fact acting in the capacity of a leader. It is crucial that you grasp the difference between *this notion* and the concept of leading people or having followers.

This is why we frequently hear phrases like: a leader in the field of cognitive psychology, a leader in the field of engineering, and a leader in the field of human biology. The ones who achieve these titles are the top experts in their respective fields—i.e. their area of gifting. This shows that they have reached the top 5% in their respective fields. They have learned to maximize and serve their gift with the highest degree of potency, excellence, and efficiency and, in the process, became leaders—i.e. those in the lead in their respective disciplines.

Their designation as leaders doesn't consider if they have followers or not. Nor should it. It only considers their excellence.

The Gift of Leadership

When it comes to discussing areas of natural ability, it's essential for me to mention the specific talent of leadership or the skill to lead others. But is it possible to have a natural talent for leadership?

While being a leader means to lead in an area of gifting, I do believe there are individuals who are particularly gifted in the area of leading, directing, influencing, or managing people, whether naturally or as a gift of the Holy Spirit.

The Scripture says (concerning spiritual gifts given to believers):

"In his grace, God has given us different gifts for doing certain things well. So if God has given you the ability to prophesy, speak out with as much faith as God has given you. If your gift is serving others, serve them well. If you are a teacher, teach well. If your gift is to

encourage others, be encouraging. If it is giving, give generously. ***If God has given you leadership ability, take the responsibility seriously.*** *And if you have a gift for showing kindness to others, do it gladly."* ~Roman 12:6-8, NLT

Although there is undoubtedly a spiritual gift of leadership among believers, I also think that some individuals have a natural talent in the same area, regardless of their belief. Typically, we refer to these individuals as naturally gifted or born leaders.

However, I acknowledge that this belief is not widely respected and may provoke controversy.

Honestly, in a room with ten leadership experts or gurus, you would probably have at least 9 out of 10 (if not all) who would say that leaders are made, not born (or genetically inclined/naturally gifted).

This is a grave fallacy in the field of leadership studies. It is just as silly as saying that all of those who excel in their respective field learned it strictly through training and/or studying.

Riddle me this: where did Babe Ruth get his ability to hit baseballs? Or Mozart obtain his ability to compose and play music. Or Mark Twain his ability to write? Or Michelangelo his ability to sculpt/paint? I surmise that no amount of training can make someone great at something if he isn't already naturally gifted to some degree in the beginning.

Leading people, in my opinion, is no exception.

Furthermore, why would God bother with ascribing talents or spiritual gifts if we could just learn to do something? He could just give inner conviction to someone, and that would be enough. Each time, the individual would improve and reach a position of prominence.

Are Leaders Born or Made?

In leadership development and studies, the common belief is that "leaders are not born, but made." Some people argue, tongue in cheek, that we are all born as babies, not as leaders. Those who support this belief assert that no one is naturally born a leader and that we can all cultivate leadership qualities by focusing on personal development, dedication, training, and making a deliberate choice. Unfortunately, this bears an uncanny resemblance to… *ideological communism.*

Nevertheless, a great majority in the field of leadership espouse that notion that *anyone* can become a good leader with enough training, motivation, effort, and dedication. Well, if you've bought into this narrative, perhaps it's time to consider this saying by Roman emperor Marcus Aurelius:

"Don't worry about siding for or against the majority. Worry about taking up any of their irrational beliefs."

Indeed, the belief (that leaders aren't born but made) has become so widespread within the realm of leadership studies, it risks bordering on irrationality if left unexamined. I am thus hoping this book will provide my readers with a much-needed new insight on the topic. I hope it allows you to reexamine your previous teachings on leadership and discover a fresh perspective that ignites hope and revitalizes your pursuit of your calling and leadership development.

As much as I respect many of those who embrace and teach this philosophy, I disagree with it. I realize, however, that disagreeing with such a popular notion requires that I provide strong argumentation to prove my point. This I will certainly attempt.

So, can leaders be made? Certainly. Does motivation and personal growth play a part in leadership excellence? Of course. But not all of those who are motivated will excel. Just because you study in a field doesn't guarantee you'll be at the top of your class. Just consider how motivated the entrants in the popular TV show *American Idol* are when they wait for hours on end just to get their shot at being America's next singing sensation. Nobody can deny their high degree of motivation, drive, and even training in some cases. Nevertheless, rare are those who get the nod of approval from Simon Cowell. Catch my drift?

Paul Okum, author of the excellent Kindle book *Leadership DNA*, had this to say on whether leaders (of people) are born or made:

"Whether as DNA from biological parents, a gift from God, or both, the clear minority argument in this debate is that we are each born with a unique set of attributes or talents, and consequently, not everyone will possess leadership ability. Accordingly, leadership cannot be learned and bolted on to everyone. As a former director of human resources for twenty-three years for an organization within the U.S. Department of Defense, I had the opportunity to observe and analyze hundreds of individuals in leadership positions and thereby

witness firsthand the effects of the popular argument that leaders can be made. My own personal experiences as a leader of a workforce of 105 employees and my observations and interactions with team leaders, supervisors, managers, and military officers in leadership positions in other organizations have forced me to the conclusion that the currently accepted premise that anyone can be a leader is utterly false and the main cause of the poor leadership in America."

I wholeheartedly agree with Mr. Okum's position. Many leadership failings have occurred because of this prevalent belief that leadership ability can be taught to anyone. The truth is, those who are exceptional at leading people often possess an innate talent or aptitude for it.

The Brain of Leaders

It might surprise you, but studies have proven that there are significant variations in the brains of individuals skilled in leadership compared to others.

The discoveries in neuroplasticity and brain evolution through autosuggestion and training pose an interesting question. Do leaders have different brains due to training or genetics? It's the chicken or the egg question.

Personal growth expert Stephen Covey addressed this, saying, *"Are leaders born or made? This is a false dichotomy—leaders are neither born nor made. Leaders choose to be leaders."*

I would also add to the above observation, *"Leaders choose to be leaders [...] as they embrace their individual calling and its associated challenges."*

For sure, an undeniable measure of intentionality goes into one's leadership development. And by making that choice, I think we can modify and shape our brain-wave patterns through consistent conditioning and training; like our bodies. However, individual brains possess distinct DNA and pre-determining qualities, also like our bodies. These predetermining qualities, I believe, can either make of break would-be leaders of people.

As in many existing skill sets, leadership capacity or talent can be graded on a bell curve. It looks something like this:

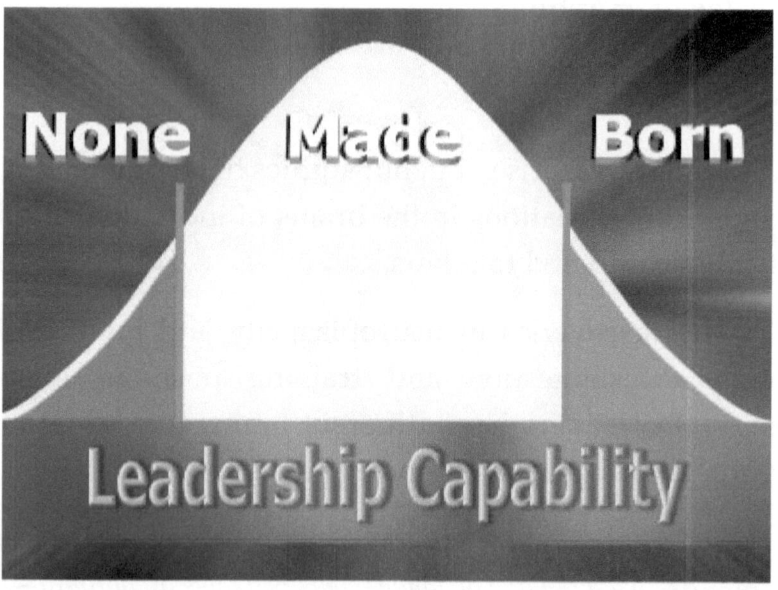

The above bell curve graphic adequately represents leadership ability distribution among segments of people.

At the beginning of the curve (under *none*), we have those who possess little to no ability *to lead others*. No amount of training, reading of books, or seminars could make these people good or efficient *at leading people*. It's just not their bent. It's not their calling, and they are simply not wired for it. Keep in mind this doesn't mean they cannot *lead in the area of their gift*. It just means that they wouldn't be able to lead ants at a picnic—and so, much less, people.

At the other end of the curve (under *born*), we have the portion of the population who are natural or born leaders (of people). These are the strong, charismatic, visionary, and naturally gifted leaders—*born leaders*. These types are good at leading people *naturally*—the same way some are naturally gifted at hitting a baseball.

Now, the error in the field of leadership training is that they took the middle portion, which includes the larger portion of people who can be made into adequate to good leaders, and applied it to *all people*. This is why the prevailing belief in leadership studies is that leaders can be developed. You see, within the high percentage of *leaders that can be made*, some will be made to excel, and some will be made to be merely adequate. In other words, results may vary depending on many factors. These 'made leaders' are the people whose brain circuitry is tweaked advantageously through training and conditioning. However, the ratio of *truly great leaders* isn't found in that portion of the bell curve. The highest attainment, rather, is found in individuals who possess innate leadership qualities and actively pursue the enhancement of their people skills, training, leadership knowledge, and personal growth.

These are the leaders who are said to have different brains from the get-go—the *Joshuas* and the *Moses* of the world in whom is found both leadership ability and a 'spirit of leadership'.

Research on leaders' brains has found increased neuro-connections in the pre-frontal cortex compared to average individuals. Additionally, their serotonin production levels are said to be higher. It's interesting to highlight that serotonin is the brain chemical that triggers leadership.

World-renowned leadership trainer Simon Sinek called serotonin "the leadership chemical". Individuals with high serotonin production are known for their ability to thrive in high-pressure situations. Serotonin plays a role in naturally regulating your mood. When your serotonin levels are good, you feel:

- Happier
- Calmer
- More focused
- Less anxious
- Emotionally stable

Studies also found that people with depression often have low levels of serotonin. It could therefore be argued that people whose brain produces more serotonin have a distinct advantage over others when it comes to *leading people*, which requires a level head, collectedness, and being cool under pressure. These traits are not commonly found in everyone, regardless of what we are told or wish for. The widespread belief in this teaching (that leaders are made, not born) is a result of a mentality that undermines excellence, and it has affected our society for decades. It's called leveling down. It's the toxic 'let's give everybody a trophy' for participating philosophy. As much as some may disagree, the fact is that not everybody can be made into a good leader (of people).

While this is a fact, don't let it discourage you. As this book will progressively and aptly demonstrate, this truth by no means disqualifies you from being a leader (of your gift).

Joshua and the Spirit of Leadership

In the book of Numbers, in the Bible, we read a very interesting account. Moses, one of history's greatest leaders, is pleading with Yahweh to have his successor appointed to lead Israel:

"Moses said to the Lord, "May the Lord, the God who gives breath to all living things, appoint someone over this community to go out and come in before them, one who will lead them out and bring them in, so the Lord's people will not be like sheep without a shepherd."

So the Lord said to Moses, "Take Joshua son of Nun, <u>a man in whom is the spirit of leadership</u>, and lay your hand on him." ~Numbers 27:15-18, NIV

In this passage, Joshua is singled out by God to take over the leadership of the nation of Israel because he is said to have *'the spirit of leadership.'*

What does this mean, exactly? Well, to shed more light on the topic, let's consider other Bible translations of that verse (Numbers 27:18).

The King James puts it this way, *"And the Lord said unto Moses, take thee Joshua the son of Nun, a man in whom is the spirit, and lay thine hand upon him."*

Several other popular translations render it as *'the spirit'* as well. The ESV, the NKJV, the NASB, and the RSV all use 'the spirit'.

The Contemporary English Version (CEV) provides an interesting twist with this rendition: *"Joshua... who can do the job..."*

Firstly, I do not believe *the spirit of leadership* in this passage is the same as *the spiritual gift of leadership* found in the New Testament (Romans 12:8). Within that passage, Paul talks about the specific gift of the Holy Spirit for leading the Church — *the Ekklesia.*

Second, I also do not believe 'the spirit' here refers to The Holy Spirit. During Old Testament times, men did not yet have the constant ministry of the Holy Spirit. Furthermore, God doesn't say that Joshua has *His spirit* (i.e. The Holy Spirit), does He? No. He simply says he has 'the spirit'. I believe this is similar to what God said of David, calling him, *'a man after my own heart'* (1 Samuel 13:14). Meaning, a man who will strive to do what He requires. In essence, it is Yahweh saying, *"Take Joshua the son of Nun, a man in whom is the spirit [I am looking for], and lay thine hand upon him.*

Third, there's a captivating English expression that employs the word 'spirit' in a unique manner. When we say that someone has 'spirit', what do we mean? For instance, if I say, *"He may be short, but he sure has spirit!"* The expression offers a way of saying that someone has what it takes: courage, determination, to do a task.

In fact, the exact definition of 'spirit' in this context is interesting.

Collins dictionary defines it this way: *spirit* is the courage and determination that helps people to survive in difficult times and to keep their way of life and their beliefs. Ex: She was a very brave girl and everyone who knew her admired her spirit. Thus, one could surmise that Yahweh acknowledged Joshua's courage and determination to assist Israel in surviving the forthcoming difficult times, all the while preserving their way of life and beliefs.

Fourth, and most obvious, I believe God singled out Joshua largely for his *natural leadership ability*. Joshua was clearly a born, gifted, and natural leader (of people). This much is obvious in Scripture. It was an integral part of his persona, skills, and abilities. So, God's mention of Joshua's *spirit of leadership* is, at least in part, a recognition of his innate leadership abilities. And when someone who has this leadership ability uses it, guess what usually happens? People follow. Yahweh still wished for his people to have a human shepherd, after Moses, who could lead them through the challenges that awaited them.

So, we understand the Most High singled Joshua out because of his leadership ability, but is that all there is to it? Is there nothing more to this concept of "spirit of leadership"? Is that all He saw in Joshua? An innate ability to lead people? Oh, no. That's just the cherry on the sundae, the icing on the cake—or the tip of the iceberg. There's more, much more to Joshua and his *spirit of leadership* than a mere ability to lead people. God knew it. He also knew that, in some other cases, *the spirit of leadership* may or may not be accompanied by an ability to lead people.

Are you shocked by this assertion? Don't be.

Let's unpack this further, shall we?

Here is an interesting question to consider…

As the appointed leader, and one who had *"the spirit of leadership"*, was Joshua concerned with having the Israelite people follow him? Surprisingly, the answer can be both "yes and no" or possibly "not necessarily".

We understand more about *the spirit of leadership* by reading more about the life, attitudes, and exploits of Joshua. As we do, we learn that the spirit of leadership, whether in Joshua or others, doesn't concern itself with how many people follow. In fact, we could even surmise that the very opposite is true. The spirit of leadership will sharpen someone's will to the degree that they're wiling to stand alone as they face their calling and all adversity that may relate to it.

This is exactly who Joshua was. He was a man willing to stand alone. I believe this has more to do with *the spirit of leadership* than his natural ability to lead others—although, in his case, both were required.

In the book of Joshua, in chapter 24, Joshua gathers the people of Israel to set the record straight. He gives them a prophetic and inspiring speech. For the first 13 verses, he reminds them about everything they've been through, and how

The Lord has been with them. But he also mentions that while God was always faithful, they were not. And so, in verses 14 and 15, he takes a bold and lone stand, saying:

"Now therefore fear the Lord, and serve him in sincerity and in truth: and put away the gods which your fathers served on the other side of the flood, and in Egypt; and serve ye the Lord. And if it seem evil unto you to serve the Lord, choose you this day whom ye will serve; whether the gods which your fathers served that were on the other side of the flood, or the gods of the Amorites, in whose land ye dwell: **_but as for me and my house, we will serve the Lord._***"* ~Joshua 24:14-15, KJV

With those final words, Joshua drew a definite line in the sand. He was, in effect, saying, *"I don't care if you follow me or not. Today, I am taking a stand. As for me and my house, we will serve the Lord."*

That's the spirit of leadership in action!

It's not about the followers, the crowd, the accolades, or the fanfare. It's about the inner fortitude to stand for something with all your mind, heart, and soul—come hell or high water.

Embracing the spirit of leadership in the age of influence and narcissism is the focus of this book's subtitle.

You see, influence and narcissism are concerned about followers and accolades. The spirit of leadership isn't. In a later chapter, I tackle the marked differences between both influence and leadership. Even though they are two very different animals, they are often used interchangeably.

Those who, like Joshua, have embraced and honed a genuine *spirit of leadership* possess three distinct characteristics:

1. They have discovered their gift (talents, abilities, calling, divine assignment, purpose).

2. They are willing to do whatever it takes to develop it and share it with the world.

3. They don't care if anyone follows.

So, a question you need to ask yourself is: have I truly embraced *the spirit of leadership* in my life, or have I focused my efforts on becoming better at the traditional concept of leadership—concerned over having followers in the process?

Make no mistake, embracing *the spirit of leadership* is far more challenging than it seems, and it will test your mettle. As Hans F. Hansen observed, *"It takes nothing to join the crowd. It takes everything to stand alone."*

Leadership vs. The Spirit of Leadership

Let's delve further into the differences between traditional leadership understanding and the spirit of leadership. You'll notice that they are completely distinct.

- Leadership makes you a leader *of* men. The spirit of leadership makes you a leader *among* men.

- Leadership makes you value people as you guide them. The spirit of leadership makes you valuable for people as you guide yourself.

- Leadership requires selflessness. The spirit of leadership requires selfless independence.

- Leadership requires teamwork to make the dream work. The spirit of leadership requires work and divine intervention to make the dream work.

- Leadership may make you weary of people and/or worried. The spirit of leadership may make you wary of people and/or worried.

- Leadership may well get you promoted. The spirit of leadership offers no guarantees.

- Leadership enables you to give meaningful direction to others. The spirit of leadership enables you to give meaningful direction to yourself.

- Leadership says to others, 'Let's go!' The spirit of leadership says to oneself, 'Just do it.'

- Leadership inspires others *to follow you*. The spirit of leadership inspires others *to emulate you*.

- Leadership requires followers to be validated. The spirit of leadership doesn't require followers. Period.

Terms of Contention

One of the biggest stigmas associated with leadership is the fact that the word itself has been mostly associated with social, political, corporate, or business settings.

The 'corporate', positional, or 'higher office' stigma associated with the word *leadership* has convinced many otherwise strong, capable, and inspiring people to disqualify themselves altogether from seeing their own worth as leaders.

The term 'leader' should thus be reevaluated as it can undermine individuals without followers, platforms, or positions, even if they have accomplished great things.

Years ago, Dr. Myles Munroe received an invitation to speak at a Christian leadership seminar. Despite the anticipation of hundreds attending, only a few individuals showed up that evening. Seeing this, he opened his presentation by saying:

"Having spoken worldwide on this topic many times, the low turnout tonight doesn't faze or shock me at all. In fact, I expected it. Why? Well, in my experience, when delivering a motivational talk or otherwise teaching on a wide range of topics, individuals tend to relate. They feel it has to do with their own lives. But when it comes to the particular subject of leadership, most people don't feel like it's for them. They don't see themselves as leaders. As a result, they don't feel like the topic of leadership applies to them. So, they fail to show up."

He continued, *"You see, this is a result of social conditioning. We are trained to think that leaders are individuals who hold positions of authority or wear fancy business attire. We are educated to view politicians and higher officials as leaders. But what we are never taught is that there is a leadership call on our own lives. We are seldom educated about the fact that all humans have an inherent leadership mandate and responsibility. Consequently, there have been multiple instances where individuals have excused themselves when I brought up the topic of leadership—such as tonight.*

The social conditioning he was talking about is that leadership has always been equated with the ability to *lead people,* and I understand why most can't identify with it. As we have seen, it's just not for everybody.

We will, however, uncover many more layers of leadership than this lone attribute. As we progress in this book, I will elucidate further the distinct differences between these eight terms related to leadership. These are:

- **Personal leadership:** The inner fortitude that pushes an individual to be decisive and intentional about leading his own life instead of accepting it. It is also coupled with strong character, moral rectitude, and daily decisiveness that leads to intentional, daily, and purposeful action.

  Followers required to qualify: none

- **Leadership in an area of gifting (of your gift/talent):** The self-knowledge and passion which enables an individual to find their particular gift, to develop it, and to serve it with purpose, quality, quantity, conscientiousness, and thus affecting people and possibly even history in the process—whether in their lifetime of afterwards.

  Followers required to qualify: none

- **Thought leadership:** Thought leaders are the informed opinion leaders and the go-to people in their respective field of expertise, or area of gifting. A thought leader is someone whose views on a subject may be taken to be authoritative, innovative, and/or influential. They are usually trusted sources who move and inspire people through innovative ideas (thoughts); and who often have a knack to turn those ideas into reality as proof. That said, one whose thoughts are not yet known or published can also be a thought leader, albeit an unrecognized one, simply because his ideas or concepts are exploring or breaking new ground.

Followers required to qualify: some (and in some cases, none)

- **Leadership ability:** This is a special ability that enables an individual to develop trust in others by demonstrating outstanding knowledge, people skills and competence in the areas of managing, decision making, guiding, motivating and empowering people in pursuing a course of action or direction that leads to a given goal, purpose, or vision. Simply put, it is a particular talent/ability to lead people.

  Leadership ability is how people have traditionally perceived and understood leadership, defining it for generations.

  Followers required to qualify: some

- **Positional leadership:** A leadership title bestowed upon an individual often regardless of his gifts, skills, or abilities which empowers him to tell others what to do through authority in order to attain a goal, reach a destination, or complete a vision which is not his own. Managers, bosses, and supervisors are found in this category.

Followers required to qualify: none

- **Influence:** A particular capacity which enables an individual to have an effect on the character, development, thoughts and actions of someone or something. Influence with people is factored on the three pillars of being known, liked, and trusted. It also rests on at least one of the following to be in effect: *charisma, knowledge, accomplishment, competence, or passion.*

Followers required to qualify: some

- **The spiritual gift of leadership:** According to Peter C. Wagner, author of *Your Spiritual Gifts Can Help Your Church Grow*, the spiritual gift of leadership is: *"The special ability that God gives to certain members of the body of Christ to set goals in accordance with God's purpose for the future and to communicate these goals to others in such a way that they voluntarily and harmoniously work together to accomplish these goals for the glory of God."* The main difference between this and secular 'Leadership Ability' listed above, is that this particular gift *is given to the believers by the Holy Spirit* at the new birth, or perhaps afterward. Also, it is magnified for use within ministry towards other believers and for the glory of God. That said, those endowed with this gift can certainly exercise it in secular pursuits as well.

Followers required to qualify: some

- **Popularity/Fame:** The state or condition of being liked, admired, known, or supported by a large number of people. Fame has very little to do with actual leadership of any kind, and everything to do with followership through some form of influence. Nevertheless, with today's widespread lack of discernment, many have misconstrued it for a leadership quality. Popularity, in its purest sense, is merely *perceived* value—not genuine value.

Followers required to qualify: many

These various terms, which are frequently used interchangeably in the field of leadership development, cause much confusion. Clearly, they are *NOT* the same. But defining these *terms of contention* serves to explain why so much angst occurs over having followers to feel validated.

Indeed, notice how four of the above terms (50%) intrinsically require followers to be authenticated; they are: *leadership ability, influence, the spiritual gift of leadership, and popularity.*

As for positional leadership, the leader makes the position and thus may or may not gather followers during his tenure. Some are good positional leaders, while some others can be horrendous.

Note, however, how *personal leadership, leadership in an area of gifting,* and to a large extent, *thought leaders,* does not require many followers to be substantiated. These three elements encapsulate the core of authentic leadership. But, interestingly, they have very little to do with *having followers*. Furthermore, when these traits are combined and actively exercised through purpose-driven intent, they coalesce to form the very *spirit of leadership* in a person.

This truth is so powerful that you could stop reading here and it would probably be enough to effect positive change in your life. Nevertheless, by all means, I urge you to read on.

People Flock to Gifts, Not to Leaders

Followers are just a bunch of *flockers*. No, seriously. A very limited number of followers actually follow a leader for the person he is. By the way, this is not a fault; it is just a fact dictated by human nature.

The Scriptures provide an excellent example of how followers, more often than not, will follow a leader not for his vision, personality, or strength of character, *but for what they can get from him.* Consider this example from the ministry of Jesus:

"On the following day, when the people who were standing on the other side of the sea saw that there was no other boat there, except that one which His disciples had entered, and that Jesus had not entered the boat with His disciples, but His disciples had gone away alone—however, other boats came from Tiberias, near the place where they ate bread after the Lord had given thanks— when the people therefore saw that Jesus was not there, nor His disciples, they also got into boats and came to Capernaum, seeking Jesus. And when they found Him on the other side of the sea, they said to Him, "Rabbi, when did You come here?"

Jesus answered them and said," Most assuredly, I say to you, you seek Me, not because you saw the signs, but because you ate of the loaves and were filled. Do not labor for the food which perishes, but for the food which endures to everlasting life, which the Son of Man will give you, because God the Father has set His seal on Him." ~John 6:22-27, NKJV

Jesus knew that these followers, even if they called Him Rabbi (teacher), wanted to fill their bellies more than their minds and hearts. Human being are egotistical creatures. They almost always operate on a 'what's in it for me' mentality. As such, they often follow someone out of shallow, superficial, self-serving, or ignorant motives.

The true disciples of Jesus, however, were following Him for the right reasons. We discover in the same chapter that, despite sharing challenging teachings, they remained steadfast while others deserted Him.

"From that time many of His disciples went back and walked with Him no more. Then Jesus said to the twelve, "Do you also want to go away?" But Simon Peter answered Him, "Lord, to whom shall we go? You have the words of eternal life. Also we have come to believe and know that You are the Christ, the Son of the living God." ~John 6:66-69, NKJV

Interestingly, the truest gift of Jesus wasn't His miracles. Sure, His miracles were spectacular signs to authenticate who He was, and Jesus expected them to stir people into becoming disciples. But His real gift, while on earth, was His person—who He was and what His presence on earth meant. Those who understood this, even if in small part or imperfectly, followed Him whether He provided bread or not.

Similarly, followers typically seek the leader's gift. For example, those who follow Tony Robbins do so because his gift for teaching principles that can improve their quality of life is remarkable. Those who follow LeBron James do so because of his gift for handling a basketball. Those who follow Gordon Ramsay do so because of his gift for cooking masterpieces of deliciousness. And so on and so forth. Take those gifts away, and the followers will just stop following. That is just the way of the leader/follower dynamic.

The Purpose of Your Gifts

As mentioned earlier, God gave each human being a particular set of talents, gifts, strengths, and abilities. If we are to lead our lives in a proper way, we are to be good stewards of those special gifts by becoming fruitful through their good use.

In the parable of the talents, for example, we are given a very clear picture of what God expects of us when we are entrusted with talents. By the way, in the parable, the word 'talent' is a monetary unit of Jesus' time—which is more than fitting when put in context with the meaning of the story. I have taught it myself from a monetary standpoint because I believe the lessons have a lot to do with how to handle finances.

That said, it can also be understood from a standpoint of how we manage our natural abilities as well—case in point, our talents. In any case, I think a re-reading of the story is necessary, so I included it here:

"For the kingdom of heaven is like a man traveling to a far country, who called his own servants and delivered his goods to them. And to one he gave five talents, to another two, and to another one, to each according to his own ability; and immediately he went on a journey. Then he who had received the five talents went and traded with them, and made another five talents. And likewise he who had received two gained two more also. But he who had received one went and dug in the ground, and hid his lord's money. After a long time the lord of those servants came and settled accounts with them.

"So he who had received five talents came and brought five other talents, saying, 'Lord, you delivered to me five talents; look, I have gained five more talents besides them.' His lord said to him, 'Well done, good and faithful servant; you were faithful over a few things, I will make you ruler over many things. Enter into the joy of your lord.' He also who had received two talents came and said, 'Lord, you delivered to me two talents; look, I have gained two more talents besides them.' His lord said to him, 'Well done, good and faithful servant; you have been faithful over a few things, I will make you ruler over many things. Enter into the joy of your lord.'

"Then he who had received the one talent came and said, 'Lord, I knew you to be a hard man, reaping where you have not sown, and gathering where you have not scattered seed. And I was afraid, and went and hid your talent in the ground. Look, there you have what is yours.'

"But his lord answered and said to him, 'You wicked and lazy servant, you knew that I reap where I have not sown, and gather where I have not scattered seed. So you ought to have deposited my money with the bankers, and at my coming I would have received back my

own with interest. Therefore take the talent from him, and give it to him who has ten talents.

'For to everyone who has, more will be given, and he will have abundance; but from him who does not have, even what he has will be taken away. And cast the unprofitable servant into the outer darkness. There will be weeping and gnashing of teeth.'" ~Matthew 25:14-30, NKJV

So, in this parable, we learn the following lessons about God's economy and purpose for the use of our gifts:

- **We are all entrusted with a differing number of talents.** Some are given a single one, some are given many, but…

- **We are all expected to become fruitful.** God expects us to exercise our talents and bear fruit in our lives as a result. This will not only bless the user himself, but others as well. Furthermore, being fruitful also glorifies the Master—God, our Creator and King.

- **God will only add more measure where He witnesses growth.** In other words, blessings and growth will flow more abundantly to those who apply those principles than to those who 'hide their talents'. Let it be added that your growth, in God's economy, may or may not include followers.

The Lord is very serious about this last point. For instance, in the parable of the talents, He took away from the 'lazy servant' who bore no fruit and gave it to the one who bore the most fruit. This is how the Father manages His business—His

Kingdom. This is how He governs. Like any good government, he wants *productive* citizens. He even equipped them with gifts in order for them to bear fruit. These gifts are our natural talents or our spiritual gifts. Picasso, the Italian painter, understood this principle when he said:

"The meaning of life is to find your gift. The purpose of life is to give it away." ~Pablo Picasso

In his interpretation, the late psychiatrist, author, and media personality, David Viscott, added to Picasso's quote by enhancing it in the middle. He said, *"The purpose of life is to discover your gift. The work of life is to develop it. The meaning of life is to give your gift away."*

It's crucial not to underestimate the significance of working on your gift, developing it. Someone who leads his own life well will understand and apply this simple principle of *talent stewardship*. At the heart of leadership is the act of guiding oneself and honing one's unique abilities.

Your Mission's Statement

Budding entrepreneurs, innovators, creators, and leaders are often told how important it is to write down their mission statement in a clear and concise manner. It serves as a blueprint and keeps them on point.

A mission statement is defined as *"a formal summary of the aims and values of a company, organization, or individual"*. This is something that I have done, and believe me, defining it clearly is not as easy as it sounds. Regardless of their field, every leader needs to do this because a mission statement should be linked to their purpose in life and work on earth.

Your *mission's statement*, however, focuses on demonstrating your mission clearly through your life and ensuring others understand it.

Your vision or goal as a leader should be bigger than you. The way you live should be a reflection of it.

In order to have loyal followers, they must want to follow the ideas you set, the vision you see, and the goals you march towards. In that sense, your *mission's statement* speaks louder than your *mission statement*. Your mission statement is made up of mere words. Your mission's statement is made alive through you and through the successive actions you take on a daily basis.

As a human being, a mission, something that surpasses your own self, is the answer you're looking for.

Leaders are merely people who have found their mission and fell in love with it. They deeply care about *something*. This is what energizes them past any hurdle—whether they have followers or not.

Friedrich Nietzsche was right when he observed, *"He who has a 'why' to live for can bear almost any 'how'."*

Good Leaders vs. Great Leaders

It was American business writer Tom Peters, who said: *"Good leaders create followers; great leaders create other leaders."*

As you reach of the conclusion of this first powerful chapter, I hope you see why leadership needs to be redefined.

The great leaders throughout history were more concerned with WHO followed them than with how many followed them. They were more concerned with quality than quantity. They wanted to reproduce themselves in others and were selective of who they chose to mentor. Their goal was to improve those who interacted with them, making them better than they were before. Their aim was to create new leaders who would continue a legacy of their own.

That's an intrinsic part of *the spirit of leadership*.

Now, let me ask you…

Are you a *good* leader, or a *great* one?

CHAPTER 2

Why You Don't Have Followers... Yet

"Leadership doesn't require having 12, 12,000, or 12,000,000 followers–in fact, real leadership often begins with 0 followers, and a whole lot of people telling you that you're an idiot."

~Dustin McKissen

This chapter, I believe, will undoubtedly set the tone for the rest of the book. Exploring the reasons behind the failure of some renowned thinkers, creators, or doers to attract a following is essential.

So, in a way, this chapter is *a study of failure*.

I believe that understanding the dynamics of failure itself serves to differentiate between the person (the leader) and his results (or lack thereof). To a considerable extent, this entire book examines the overarching theme that *failing doesn't make you a failure*.

The Kolbrin, also known as *The Kolbrin Bible*, is an interesting book consisting of ancient texts. Much like the Bible, it comprises multiple writings divided into two main parts. The first section contains what is commonly called 'the wisdom of the Egyptians', while the second part consists of Celtic texts dating back to the time of the New Testament. The book has much to offer in terms of history, morals, wisdom and, yes, even *leadership*. With that said, I wish to bring this passage to your attention, for it expresses the exact overarching sentiment of this chapter:

"The greatest men have no memorial if their endeavors were unpopular or not crowned with success. For every great man with a memorial, there are a thousand unknown and unhonored." ~The Kolbrin, Book of Morals and Precepts, 6:12

While I wholeheartedly dedicated this book to my more-than-deserving wife, I also had those thousands (more like millions) of unknown and unhonored men and women in mind when I typed every single keystroke in this book.

Indeed, this work is my heart's cry for all those whose momentous efforts went unnoticed, unappreciated, or were forgotten. I understand your plight. I've lived it. Believe me, I know of its sting. But I also know this is not the end of your story… nor of my own.

Regardless, these are the individuals I wrote for. I wrote it for those who dared to put it all on the line, and who later, looking back, wondered 'why?'. Why didn't I succeed? Why did I lose so much? Why is it so hard?

In all sincerity, I wish I could give a specific and constructive answer to help every single one of you. But, alas, I too am still looking for answers. So, this book is the product of my imperfect journey to comprehend why so many fail and so few succeed.

In that respect, this book is just one among many that examines the ramifications of success and failure. I just happen to have a very specific audience. Among my audience are leaders without followers who carry bruises, scars, and in some cases embitterment. They possess extensive experience, knowledge, and seasoning. They went to the carnival, spent everything in attempting to win a prize, but returned empty-handed.

A Call to Introspection

While you find yourself pondering the problem of not having any followers, whether it is real or imagined, you must be willing to look at yourself in the mirror objectively. A season experiencing a lack of followers may not be because of outside, adversarial, or unknown forces. Self-candor, therefore, is essential to reflect on the possibility that you, and you alone, could be the problem (?).

But even if the evidence points to you, don't be too hard on yourself. In fact, join the club! Everybody has issues they need to address, or character flaws they need to redress.

So, in order to address and redress those issues, you must take a long, profound look at yourself. You must engage in a willful exercise in introspection. You must learn to resolve the conflicts within before facing the conflicts without. Or, as someone once put it, *"If you don't go within, you will go without."*

To that end, ask yourself these vital questions:

- How is my overall leadership *ability (to lead people)*?
- How well do I relate to others?
- What is it like to be on the other side of me?
- How disciplined am I?
- How much value do I *really* bring to the table?
- What have I done with my gifts?

Taking an honest look at yourself as a leader is the first step in assessing the 'WHY?' of any predicament. Truthfully, 85% of *leaders without followers* are such because of who they are and/or what they do (or fail to do)—whether good or bad. Let me stress here that not having followers, depending on where you are on your journey, is perhaps not your fault at all or even a negative thing. As we have seen earlier, it most likely is a temporary setback.

However, whether you're responsible for your lack of followers or not, refusing to take any responsibility speaks volumes about who should be blamed.

Furthermore, before attempting any hasty diagnosis about reasons for followership or lack thereof, any aspiring leader, seasoned leader, or student of leadership should answer the following questions:

- Am I someone worthy of being followed?
- If so, why?

These are brutally honest questions you must ask yourself.

We All Begin Without Followers

In the Bible, Job expresses a sobering thought which applies to all of us. Distressed after his massive losses, he laments: *"Naked I came from my mother's womb, and naked shall I return."* ~Job 1:21, ESV

Just like our physical birth, our journey towards leadership and purpose often begins with us being naked, alone, and lacking resources.

I like Simon Sinek's keen observation about this part of the leadership journey. He said: *"Leaders don't convince people to follow them. Leaders walk forward alone and those who want to go down their path decide to follow."*

Regardless of the field or people we aim to influence with our skills, enthusiasm, product, or expertise, we all must begin somewhere—typically on our own. Many leaders without followers are in that position because they are new to their role. They've only just begun and are merely in warm-up mode. Maybe that's you.

It is normal to have few or no followers during the start-up phase of any endeavor. At the beginning, your fanbase might mainly consist of friends and family. It may even be just your mother, if you're lucky. This is something you should anticipate, regardless of your potential impact or talents. Relax, there's no reason to be concerned. It's all part of the journey as a budding leader.

The simple fact that you're taking your first steps suffices to explain why you may lack followership. Nonetheless, this single denominator is not the only thing that accounts for why you feel like you're merely taking a walk.

Ten Reasons Why You May Have No Followers

The dynamics between leadership and followership are complex. A one-size-fits-all explanation for why you or I may have no followers is not realistic at all. In this chapter, I explore the reasons that could explain why you don't have any followers yet. As you read, keep in mind that being successful in your calling may not even require having followers.

No matter what the circumstances are, my suggestion is to go through each potential reason and make a note of the ones that strongly resonate with your individual situation.

So, here are *ten reasons* that may explain away your lonely walk, along with some potential solutions:

1- You are a lone wolf

Wolves, like humans, are pack animals who function better in a more or less complex societal hierarchy in order to survive and succeed in hunting large prey. Humans, as a society, tend to disregard "lone wolves" (also called lone rangers) as people who are quirky, odd, and more than likely incompetent or untrustworthy. Even if some wolves in nature do manage to thrive on their own as lone wolves, you will notice, are usually skinnier and weaker than their pack counterparts, which feed on larger prey.

Similarly, not all leaders in the human world have a friendly, outgoing personality or a sociable disposition. There are some who are either highly introverted, highly independent, or both.

Actually, leaders who prioritize their gift often have fewer followers due to their stronger passion for projects or products rather than people. Introverted leaders tend to prioritize tasks and processes over managing people, as it aligns better with their energy levels. This simply means they are not, as we have already examined earlier in our terms of contention, inclined to being *leaders of people.'* Now, this by no means implies that they are mean, unloving, or unkind with people. It just means that these *task-oriented leaders* get their batteries depleted faster around people. Conversely, it may also mean that they get their batteries charged up and are at their best when tackling thorough research or working on a project alone.

That being said, it is important to recognize that independent leaders typically experience setbacks due to their preference for working alone. Despite that, if only for the sake of personal development; people skills and cooperation are essential for any leader, even those who are more introverted and independent. And, if I may add, those are essential skills even for those who are happy with their current level of achievement. While I strongly advocate for independence throughout this book, I believe that strong independent leaders can greatly benefit from learning how to be inter-dependent leaders.

Why, you ask?

Because your legacy as a leader will probably be shaped more by the lives you touch and improve, rather than the products, ideas, or thoughts you generate.

John C. Maxwell rightly noted: *"Nothing of significance was ever achieved by an individual acting alone."*

Even the most independent leaders have others to thank for their achievements in some way, shape, or form. If we examine closely, we'll discover that there are always additional contributors—whether it's a partner, a parent, or even the inventor of a tool they utilized.

As an example, I could assert that I single-handedly wrote this book, which initially appears to be true. Nevertheless, I relied on a computer, keyboard, desk, and chair, to name just a few, to aid me in its creation. In that sense, other people who invented these useful tools find themselves as indirect contributors to my book. Do you catch my drift? So, in other words, the concept of a "self-made man" (or woman) doesn't really exist.

Although it's natural to embark on our purpose-driven leadership journey alone, it's essential to establish meaningful associations in order to make substantial progress towards our God-given purpose. After all, success is fundamentally linked to the people we know and the relationships we build.

Eventually, even the most self-sufficient leaders require a helping hand or a timely connection to move forward.

John Donne, the poet and preacher, captured this truth perfectly in his timeless words:

"No man is an island, entire of itself; every man is a piece of the continent, a part of the main. If a clod be washed away by the sea, Europe is the less, as well as if a promontory were, as well as if a manor of they friends's or of thine own were. Any man's death diminishes me, because I am involved in mankind."

In summary, no matter how much of an introverted lone wolf you may be, developing sound relationships on your leadership journey is no trivial matter. I'm not discussing followers in this context. I'm just talking about your inner circle—some people in our corner, building you up and cheering you on. These can be the deciding factor in whether or not you achieve success.

2- Your timing is wrong

"We all know that timing is everything. Trouble is, we don't know much about timing itself." ~Daniel Pink

We live in a world where everything moves so fast. It's in a constant flux of motion, change, and transformation—especially on the web marketplace. As a result, here is what I've noticed: timing is crucial for effective positioning. Indeed, as the saying goes, *timing is everything.*

Being ahead of the curve through timely action gives a significant advantage. Those who position themselves early in a fad, movement, or innovation are more likely to be perceived as leaders compared to others. These individuals establish themselves as authorities and are highly likely to succeed.

One can only refer back to the early nineties, when the *.com* revolution (aka, the birth of the internet) was in full swing. A few people saw where this was headed and wisely decided to buy a ton of .com domain names of popular brands such as McDonald's, GMC, Sony, etc. When the major corporations decided to join the online revolution, they were taken aback by the fact that their esteemed names, now with a .com attached to it, belonged to some nerd living in his parent's basement. And the rest, as they say, is history.

The same also happened for those who were smart and fast enough to position themselves when Facebook ads, live video, Instagram stories, and other such social media innovations took place. The people who were quick to run with these new online tools and platforms made a bigger splash than those who joined the parade later. A few individuals were able to achieve massive success as a result.

I often joke with Elisabeth, *"Honey, we have to find the next big thing on social media, and then leverage it."*

Of course, this is easier said than done.

Nevertheless, I must admit my wife is much better than I am at the art of timing. When it comes to having a particular conversation with someone, she always recommends the perfect moment to bring up the issue. She frequently advises, *"Just wait until 4:00 pm, when they'll have completed so and so and can give you more time."* Or, *"wait until he gets back from so and so and has done so and so, he will be more receptive.*" She consistently demonstrates a profound understanding and skillful application of timing for optimal outcomes. This has become something I rely on heavily for our business and daily tasks. She just has such a natural knack for it.

Conversely, my daughter Marissa, at the age of seven, just like most children, had very poor timing skills. Whenever I was occupied with the dishes, writing, or fixing dinner, she would often approach me to fix her broken toy or read a book. At times, it felt like she made a special effort to find me during my busiest moments just to ask for a favor. Her timing was so bad that I often joked about her needing a crash course from her mom.

Timing is a key factor in determining the success of people, projects, and leaders alike.

Just ask stand-up comedians how much the art of timing is to be honed and respected in their profession. A good stand-up comedian will know when to place a joke in his routine, what tempo should be used in his speech, as well as what is an adequate *time period* for the joke. For example, no matter how funny, a 9-11 joke would have been inappropriate within a day, a week, or even a month after the tragic events in New York City. Likewise, a leader's impact is often the result of his timing.

For instance, imagine if Martin Luther King had arrived on the scene a hundred years prior—would he have had the same lasting effect? Probably not. In fact, it is highly probable that he would have been killed much sooner and subsequently forgotten even faster. So, the same man with the same passion and the same message would have had no impact at all on history.

In Galatians 4:4-5, we read that God sent His son (Jesus):

"When the fullness of time had come, God sent forth his Son, born of woman, born under the law, to redeem those who were under the law, so that we might receive adoption as sons." (ESV)

Of course, God knew the importance of *timing* for the world's ultimate leader to show up on the scene. God sent His son *'when the fullness of time had come'*. In other words, when the timing was perfect.

Being made manifest at the right time is crucial for you too, as a leader. Your lack of followership might just be a result of your time not being ripe yet.

Many factors can impede the timing of a leader. For one, a leader can show up too soon. It is very possible for a leader to be too *avant-garde*. The world may just not be ready for their ideas, vision, or creations.

Arthur Schopenhauer said: *"Talent hits a target no one else can hit. Genius hits a target no one else can see."*

Indeed, when genius shows up, it is often too early for its own sake. As a result, very few, if any, recognize it.

This is the case of most people who became popular or famous posthumously—such as Vincent Van Gogh.

There is a poignant scene in the 2015 movie about Van Gogh's life, *At Eternity's Gate,* in which Van Gogh (played by actor Willem Dafoe), is talking with a priest and says: *"I feel like I'm painting for people who haven't been born yet."*

The Dutch painter's unwavering dedication to his unique perspective paved the way for the artistic revolution of the twentieth century. As he wrote to his brother, *"But one doesn't expect out of life what one has already learned that it cannot give, but rather one begins to see more and more clearly that life is only a kind of sowing time, and the harvest is not here."*

He painted because he felt he had to. *"I can't do anything else,"* he laments to the priest in the movie, adding, *"Believe me, I've tried."*

People called his work ugly, horrible, and terrifying. Vincent says that he paints only what he sees, what he knows. No matter his success, no matter the praise, he'd paint just the same. As sad and dramatic as this sounds, that's *the spirit of leadership* in action.

But a leader can also sometimes be *too late*. This, too, relates to timing. I often refer to this phenomenon as *'being five years late to the prom'*. This has happened to me multiple times when I would come up with a great idea for a book, message, or product, only to find out it already existed—sometimes it had existed for several months, or even years. In such cases, we just need to get back to the drawing board.

I find French poet and writer Victor Hugo's statement about the potency of well-timed ideas to be particularly interesting:

"There is nothing more powerful than an idea whose time has come."

3- You didn't position yourself properly

"Early to bed, early to rise, work like hell and advertise."
~Laurence J. Peter

Most individuals put in effort towards the first three activities described above by Canadian educator and satirist Laurence J. Peter. They're early to bed, early to rise, and they work like hell. But many fail *to present or promote their gift*–better known as *advertising*.

While this failure doesn't make them poor leaders, it sure makes them poor advertisers. And, as it stands, poor advertisers usually end up unseen, unknown, and unsung.

Later on, in a chapter titled History's Leaders Without Followers, we'll discuss some of the more well-known figures. Pay attention and you'll see a common connection throughout. The common downfall among these enthusiastic men and women was their inability to assertively market their service or product; in other words, *to position themselves.*

Of course, it was more challenging for some (especially biblical figures) since advertising may not have existed as we know it back then. However, for leaders in modern times; well, as trite as it sounds, it's on them.

In the current era, if you're a leader or entrepreneur and fail to advertise, you can pretty much blame your lack of success solely on this.

Professor of marketing and author, Steuart Henderson Britt, said:

"Doing business without advertising is like winking at a girl in the dark. You know what you are doing, but nobody else does"

Indeed, the sweetness of a tree's fruit goes unnoticed if its location remains a mystery. Don't you agree? Has God given you a gift and a passion for a product, an idea, a service, or a ministry? Tell the world about it! Shout it from the rooftops. Don't be shy.

Now, I know some of you might feel self-promoting is akin to being prideful, boastful, or lacking humility. But here is the truth: If God really did ignite your soul with a strong desire to offer a useful service or product, why should you choose to keep it to yourself? This might shock you, but in doing so, you are not acting in humility; you are being selfish. You are like the wicked servant in the parable of the talents, who goes out with his lone talent and buries it.

Why is this akin to being selfish, you ask? Because you are not making known something that could benefit your fellow man. No matter if it's apple pies, books, counseling, face creams, or oil changes, if it can aid someone in any way, it is your duty to promote it.

Interestingly, the etymology of the word 'promote' is from the Latin verb *promovere*, from *pro-* 'forward, onward' + *movere* 'to move'. So, promoting means *to move forward!*

And leadership, as we've seen, is all about forward motion.

4- You are still being prepared

In the third chapter, *Developed in The Crucible of the Darkroom*, we delve deeper into the essential preparation process that leaders often go through. So, I won't spoil it here by being too wordy.

The simple truth is, God isn't done with me; and I know He isn't done with you yet, either. As human beings, we are in a constant state of preparation for what comes next in His plan for our lives.

- Joseph was being prepared in obscurity for thirteen years to lead Egypt as its Prime Minister.
- Moses was being prepared for eighty years to lead the Israelites in the wilderness (40 as a Prince, and 40 as a shepherd).
- Jesus was being prepared for thirty years before He began His life-giving and atoning work.

And so on, and so forth.

If we don't recognize this seemingly empty period as a time for preparation, we might feel like giving up entirely. It's a common occurrence for the best of us. We must, therefore, be careful not to get discouraged. When you feel hidden from the world during these dark times, remember that patience and discernment are your most valuable allies.

5- You are too controversial

In this present age of lies, fluff, offended people, and make-believe, truth doesn't have many followers. Notice that this point is named *'you are too controversial'* and not *'you are wrong'* or *'you are promoting falsehood'*.

Many individuals don't appreciate the worth of specific concepts, services, philosophies, art, or products offered by certain leaders due to multiple factors. Accepted ideas and social trends are subject to change as culture evolves. Like the population which feeds their momentum, they too can be fickle.

According to Arthur Schopenhauer, *"All truth passes through three stages: First, it is ridiculed; second, it is violently opposed; and third, it is accepted as self-evident."*

With this in mind, guess what happens to thought-leaders whose proposed ideas, products, or mission find themselves in the first two stages of social scrutiny?

Yeah, you guessed it… not much.

And, while I don't want to be an agent of discouragement, keep in mind this phenomenon can last for years, too. So, be forewarned.

6- You are working outside of your strength zone

Sometimes a leader will focus his energies on a good, useful, and even desired project, but he may be the wrong person for the job. What I mean to say is, he may not possess the skills, knowledge, or abilities to see it through successfully. Any such endeavor will have a significantly diminished impact or may not have any impact at all. In the end, the right project in the wrong hands is the wrong project.

For example, do you remember the impact Michael Jordan had as a minor league baseball player with the Chicago White Socks?

What impact? You ask? Well, that's my point exactly.

Back on February 7, 1994, Jordan shocked the sports world by signing a minor league baseball contract with the Chicago White Sox. This experience conducted by the king of basketball is the perfect example of a leader working outside of his strength zone. To this day, experts agree that Jordan's stint into professional baseball was, sadly, very forgettable.

Nevertheless, hitting coach Mike Barnett attests he has never seen the same work ethic and dedication that Jordan showed that summer. He was a living example of working until your hands bleed. So, clearly, the problem was not linked to Jordan's work ethic. No surprise there.

Looking back, however, Barnett observed, *"You could tell, the game humbled him at that point. And that's what the game of baseball is; it's a very humbling sport. You watch him play basketball and you think he's superhuman or superman. You watch the game of baseball; it will humble you in a heartbeat."*

Obviously, although a wonderfully gifted athlete overall, Michael Jordan's clear calling and destiny was tied to basketball, not baseball. He also proved it when he returned to the Bulls in 1995, and then won three championships in a row, from 1996 to 1998.

The lesson? It doesn't matter how dedicated you are. If you are working outside your strength zone as a leader, your results will be underwhelming. Hence, the key is to know your legitimate strengths and to develop them.

7- You're preaching to the wrong crowd

Keeping in line with the previous point, there is also such a thing as working on your strengths, but aiming your efforts toward the wrong people. Trying to serve the wrong audience can have disastrous results for a leader.

As a case in point, I would like to introduce you to another author.

Lloyd Percival was a Canadian sports coach, author, and fitness guru. He trained champions in track and field, rowing, figure skating, skiing, boxing and golf. His book, *The Hockey Handbook*, first published in 1951, presented an innovative and fresh approach to training for Canada's beloved national sport. It was written specifically with hockey coaches and players in mind. Unfortunately, however, it failed to gain any traction in Canada, the NHL, and the North American hockey establishment.

Canadian hockey coaches, experts, and players found the book's content to be the strangest they had ever encountered. Breathing control? Gymnastics? Goal setting? *"No way!"* They scoffed.

Dick Irvin, the then-famous NHL coach, contemptuously called the book *"the product of a three-year-old."*

But, meanwhile, Anatoli Tarasov, the legendary Russian coach who made hockey into a mainstay in Russia, reverently referred to it as his bible.

"Your wonderful book, which introduced us to the mysteries of Canadian hockey, I have read like a schoolboy," Tarasov once told Percival.

Tarasov, of course, added his own quirks and innovations, but Percival's book was the basis of, arguably, the greatest hockey program ever created. The proof of its efficiency came especially during the famed summit series of 1972, when the prowess of Russian hockey dazed the Canadian team, but also shocked the world.

Respected around the world, Percival's controversial prescription for change turned him from a prophet without honor in his homeland and made him the stepfather of Russian hockey.

The lesson? Whatever you do, make sure you're aiming it at the right people. Or, as Jesus said: *"Do not cast your pearls before swine."* (Matthew 7:6)

8- You don't know what you need to know yet

One of the most common problems for would-be leaders is their initial lack of knowledge or know-how. If you do not yet know what you need to know, you will not go where you need to go. It's that simple.

A friend who works in finance once shared with me a story from when he was just starting his business. He found himself in a conversation with a multimillionaire who was contemplating hiring him as a financial advisor. The man asked him a certain question about hedge funds that stumped him. As a result, he lost the client. He also lost the opportunity for a very lucrative contract that would have secured his business endeavor early on.

The point is this: His then lack of knowledge on this point hindered his growth, both financially and as a leader in his field.

Knowledge and know-how, when properly expounded or demonstrated, fosters trust in others. Also, leaders who know that they know are naturally more confident. This confidence, in turn, reflects in their demeanor, and ultimately affects the confidence of would-be followers or customers.

Imagine you are at a car dealership considering their latest luxury sedan. A salesman approaches and says, *"Hi. I'm Jim. Do you have any questions about this model?"*

Then you say, *"Yes, Jim, I do. I was wondering… what is the gas mileage performance on this car?"*

"I'm not quite sure." Replies Jim, quickly adding, *"But I'm sure it's pretty good."*

Taken aback, you nonetheless ask another question, *"Um, Okay. So, what are the feature options on this model?"*

With a sly smile and confident wink, Jim answers, *"Oh, I'm not quite sure about that either. But nobody ever complains once they buy it. It offers some really good base features."*

After such an exchange, would you trust Jim and confidently buy the vehicle, or run out of the dealership? You'd probably take your business elsewhere, right? The reason is simple: Jim doesn't know diddly squat about the vehicles he's selling. He lacks knowledge, and that makes him untrustworthy.

As we develop and evolve as leaders, we improve in our unique roles and responsibilities. However, while we do so, we may experience some growing pains. Our knowledge of our craft or discipline, or lack thereof, may cause us to attract people by fostering trust, or to repel them by causing mistrust. As a result, our imperfect or limited knowledge can lead to an unsuccessful and lonely season.

The solution? Simple. Invest in self-improvement and strive for excellence in your chosen area of expertise. Aim to become part of the top 5% in your lane in knowledge expertise.

Is this easy? No.

Is it worth it? Absolutely!

9- You are being hindered/opposed

Whether we acknowledge it or not, sometimes our lack of success, recognition, or followers is really no fault of our own.

Certain individuals possess such an extraordinary gift, calling, or anointing in their field that adversaries will emerge to hinder their success.

Remember, according to the Bible, our world is governed by evil forces (John 14:30, 2 Corinthians 4:4, Ephesians 6:12).

History is replete with light-bearing individuals whose powerful gift was perceived as a threat to those in power. Often, these talented Leaders become targets in various ways - physically, legally, or spiritually. Their enemies are actively working against them to prevent them from gaining more influence. Opposition was a common thread in the lives of numerous biblical figures, including King David, Jeremiah, Nehemiah, John the Baptist, and Jesus Christ.

One example that strongly illustrates this point is the case of Nehemiah. Nehemiah had a momentous responsibility as a leader - the reconstruction of Jerusalem's wall. His work, however, didn't go unnoticed by his enemies, who plotted diligently against him day and night. Every effort was made to sabotage his undertaking. Fortunately, God had the ultimate say in this particular biblical situation.

In more recent times, the example of Nikola Tesla highlights the same predicament. Tesla's particular struggles amidst the more money-hungry sharks of his day provide a good illustration of this point. His innovations would have provided the world with *free energy*. However, those in power prevented it, which, some argue, caused Tesla's downfall.

Another story comes to mind, that of Stanley Meyer. Beginning in 1975, Stanley Meyer attempted to bring a unique idea to fruition: a car powered by his patented "water fuel cell."

For years, he worked tirelessly and even fought in the courts, until in 1998, when he was met with an untimely demise.

Stanley's brother reported that during a business meeting with potential foreign investors, Stanley began to vomit uncontrollably, claiming to have been poisoned. Meyer's cause of death, as per the coroner's report, was a cerebral aneurysm. Despite this, there are those who argue that Stanley's death was a result of poisoning.

I'll leave it up to you, the reader, to come up with your own idea about what might have happened there.

So, in such cases, when the wicked rise against you; what's the solution? While there are no guarantees, determination, faith, and prayer are your greatest allies. These can bring to pass my two favorite words in the Bible: *But God [...]*.

Indeed, a problem is always a requirement to witness a miracle. And sometimes, as leaders, a miracle is what we need. So, keep the faith and believe for miracles.

10- You lack social proof

In 2023, I indulged myself in an interesting exercise. I was looking through the Christian book section at my local Indigo bookstore, which is the largest bookstore chain in Canada. In the same section, there was a young couple in their twenties who were discussing various books, subjects, and Christian authors.

I noticed my book, *Kingdom Fundamentals: What the Kingdom of God Means, and What it Means for You*, happened to be readily available right in front of them. So, I picked it up, turned to the couple, and interrupted them, boldly saying: *"If you really want a book that will blow your mind, trust me, this is the one."*

With that said, I handed the book to the lady. They both looked at me, somewhat bewildered, as I walked over to the other side to listen in covertly for their reaction. As she flipped through the pages, I heard her say, *"Hmm, Sebastien Richard. Never heard of him."* And, just like that, she placed the book back on the shelf without giving it a second thought.

I chuckled to myself as I left their vicinity. No, I wasn't offended. Rather, I was amused. I had often heard that without social proof (of trustworthiness, notoriety, success, or widespread approval), it is exceedingly hard to get people to buy into you. I have also experienced being overlooked for that very reason many times over the years. But this particular social experiment provided me with visible and concluding evidence.

You see, followers have a herd mentality. They usually follow those they like, know, and trust. That's human nature, by the way. That's what drives us to carefully consider product reviews on Amazon before buying. There is nothing inherently wrong with that, of course. But, if you're trying to grow a business or followership, if you're not yet liked, known, or trusted, the odds are stacked against you to gain followers. This makes the climb very gradual, arduous, and steeply uphill.

It's a lot like the adage: *you need money to make money.* Well, in the same manner, *you need followers to gain followers.* Note that I didn't say here that you *need* followers to qualify as a Leader; just that you need followers to gain more influence. That's *social proof.* And social proof is what most are looking for before they decide to buy into you or, in this case, from you.

If this is you, may you find yourself encouraged by the words of poet William Wordsworth, who wrote:

"Strongest minds are often those of whom the noisy world hears least."

A Word About Entrepreneurs

I opened this chapter by talking about everyone of us beginning our journeys alone. I believe this lone stance is the necessary starting point of leadership.

One of the most powerful leadership principles is often misunderstood due to its contrarian nature. It is the following:

Leadership means finding something worth doing by yourself.

We often admire entrepreneurs in our culture. The general perception of entrepreneurs is that they are leaders. They are often considered the movers and shakers of our world, and rightly so. In fact, the word *entrepreneur* comes from the French verb: *entreprendre*. Interestingly, *entreprendre* means *'to begin something'*.

When you *begin something*, no matter what that something is, you are often alone. When you begin something that you believe in, you're often the only one who believes in it. As a result, you may have no followers to speak of. This is the reason I believe entrepreneurs are leaders in their rawest form. They are the beginners, the starter-uppers, the trailblazers. That's why a new venture is called a 'start-up'.

Once you understand *the starting point of leadership is finding something worth doing by yourself,* your view of leadership will forever be changed. It may seem counter-intuitive, but leadership does indeed start with the willingness to act independently.

We believe this notion is false because we are conditioned to understand leadership solely from the standpoint of leading people. We are led to believe, pun intended, that the words *alone* and *leadership* are an oxymoron and mutually exclusive.

When you start to broaden your perception of leaders beyond those who simply lead others, you'll truly understand the essence of leadership—*the spirit of leadership*—which is the primary theme of this book.

Followers are merely one fruit of leadership—a healthy byproduct. They are some leaders' harvest, not every leader's measure of worth.

The majority, if not all, of the greatest leaders in history embarked on their journey alone at first. Something ignited their soul, and they went after it with all their heart.

Christian missionary and author, Elisabeth Elliot, clearly understood this when she observed: *"Loneliness is a required course for leadership."*

You Are Not for Everybody

One crucial thing I learned in book writing and marketing is that effective marketing needs to both attract and repel.

As you develop your leadership, the same can be said about you. As a Leader, you will inevitably attract some people and repel others. That's a required course for leadership, and a difficult lesson. It goes against our natural desires. Naturally, we all have a preference for being liked and loved. However, we are not suited for everyone.

The Bible reminds us of this fact in regards to spiritual matters when it says: *"Our lives are a Christ-like fragrance rising up to God. But this fragrance is perceived differently by those who are being saved and by those who are perishing. To those who are perishing, we are a dreadful smell of death and doom. But to those who are being saved, we are a life-giving perfume."* ~2 Corinthians 2:15-16 (NLT)

Moreover, as you cultivate your personal leadership and fulfill your gift and calling, you will boldly champion certain beliefs. As the saying goes, *"If you don't stand for anything, you will fall for everything."* Such a bold attitude will refine and filter those who decide to follow you—to stand with you.

As individuals find their own personal leadership, they come to understand that not everyone will or should be followers. They even come to appreciate this fact.

There are many people in the world who, for various reasons, won't like you. In the same way, there are plenty of people who will genuinely care for you. These are your people—your tribe.

This point was proven by an interesting social experiment conducted some years ago.

In a New York subway, a violinist performed for 45 minutes during the morning rush. A few people paused to listen, some applauded, and he collected about $30 in tips. Not too bad, right?

Unknown to the onlookers, however, the musician was Joshua Bell, one of the finest and most celebrated violinists in the world. During this unique performance, he played some of the most complex compositions ever written. Only a few violinists worldwide are capable of adequately performing these pieces. Not only did he pull it off, but he did so on a violin valued at $3.5 million.

Just two days earlier, Bell had performed for a sold-out audience at a theater in Boston, where tickets averaged $100 each.

This subway stint was an experiment demonstrating how exceptional talent can go unrecognized in mundane settings, often undervalued and overlooked.

The lesson is simple. The world is full of unsung talent that does not receive the recognition it deserves. However, when individuals recognize their worth and find environments that appreciate their value, they flourish.

So, if your intuition sends you red flags, suggesting that your current surroundings are not right, listen to it. Seek out places where you are valued and appreciated—where your gifts are sought. Know your worth.

Save your precious time, energy, and abilities by not trying to convince the wrong people to like you. Don't waste your pearls on swine. Do not attempt to persuade them to accompany you on your journey. What's the point of wasting your time and theirs? The wrong people can cause you much harm, and the wounds they inflict may take a long time to heal. Accept that they are not for you and move on. Remain courteous while moving along on your journey, waving them by. When you share your path with someone, you are offering them a special privilege. Don't cheapen it by inviting everyone and anyone on your journey.

The sooner you assimilate this valuable lesson, the better.

The X Factor of Success

Along with Jordan Peterson and Robert Greene, Malcom Gladwell is one of my preferred secular thinkers and authors. In 2008, he wrote an interesting book titled, *Outliers: The Story of Success*.

The book discusses the reasons behind people's success. Additionally, the author proposes that successful individuals often enjoy exceptional opportunities that equally hardworking and talented individuals do not.

The thesis of the book so enthralled me, I wrote Gladwell's recipe for success, printed it, and stuck it on my office wall. I also made sure to underline the word _opportunity_, as it had been a prayer subject of mine for a while—and still is.

The key determining factors of success explored in *Outliers* form the (admittedly simplified) following equation:

Opportunity + Timing + Upbringing + Effort + Meaningful Work + Legacy =

SUCCESS!

This thesis, presented by Gladwell, mirrors what Solomon said in Ecclesiastes 9:11, which is also the epitaph for this book:

"I returned and saw under the sun that—
The race is not to the swift,
Nor the battle to the strong,
Nor bread to the wise,
Nor riches to men of understanding,
Nor favor to men of skill;
<u>*But time and chance happen to them all.*</u>*"*

Time and chance, also known as luck or opportunity, play a huge role in the success of aspiring leaders.

However, I believe there is something else involved. Something *bigger*. There's something even more mystical at work that we tend to ignore in this equation, and that is *the intervention of spiritual forces*.

Supernatural Assistance

I believe that 'divine intervention' (or divine favor) is the ultimate X factor that trumps all others when it comes to the success of an individual leader.

On the one hand, I think it's important to acknowledge the impact of true divine intervention, where God's favor reaches through time and space, influencing the right individuals along the way to help us achieve what we've worked and prayed for.

Scripture attributes many leaders' success stories to divine favor. Abraham, Joseph, Jacob, David, and numerous others were blessed by the Lord, even receiving angelic help and achieving remarkable success.

On the other hand, there are other spiritual forces at work in this world—darker ones.

If we study highly successful people, particularly those in the music and entertainment industries, for instance, we find that they also rely on higher powers for favor and success. Some of them even dare call it what it is: selling your soul to the devil.

This, dear friend, is a dark truth that most leadership and personal growth teachers will not readily admit to, or even tackle. In the game of leadership and influence, such contracts with dark forces provide an unfair advantage for a few players. In truth, most who are famous are not good, and most who are good are not famous.

George Carlin, the late stand-up comedian, was spot-on when he said of the elite, *"It's a BIG club, and you ain't in it."*

I can assure you that I'm not included in it either.

All this to say that there is, I believe, a spiritual X *factor* to be accounted for, which can explain why some make it, and why some don't.

Just like Luke Skywalker, some of you may be wondering at this point, "Is the dark side stronger?"

To that valid question, just like Yoda, I can tell you, *"No, no, no. Quicker, easier, more seductive."*

Over the past few years, I've noticed several leaders around me involved in similar situations. Their desire was to acquire more for themselves. As a result, when opportunity knocked, they blindly accepted offers they should have refused. They became successful quicker, yes, but they also became severely and visibly compromised.

On your life and leadership journey, you too might reach a crossroads where you will be required to choose. You might have to choose between partnering with the God of light or the prince of darkness for supernatural help and advancement. That choice is yours and yours alone to make, of course.

Notwithstanding, my advice is… *choose wisely.*

CHAPTER 3

Developed in the Crucible of the Darkroom

"You will become a lighthouse of personal growth and power, and by your example and leadership, you will prevent many a worthy man from crashing his life upon the rocks of mediocrity."

~Andy Andrews

The above quote by Andy Andrews, known for his bestselling inspirational books and talks, is not only inspiring but also accurate. It should, however, be accompanied by a caveat. The quote should be followed by a *"But first..."*

Indeed, before anyone can become *"a lighthouse of personal growth and power"*, there has to be a slow and often painful process through which a leader develops. An obligatory passage, if you will. That's what we'll explore in this chapter.

A few years back, Christine Caine, an evangelist and author, delivered a talk that explored the difference between *anointing* and *gifting*. During her impactful presentation, she talked about how God sometimes molds us behind the scenes before making us known to the world. She shared the crux of this talk on social media, where she wrote:

"We don't need to be discovered by God, He created us so he knows where we are. We need to be developed by Him into the likeness of Christ. He will take you into the darkroom to be developed so that the spotlight of man won't destroy you. He is more concerned that the light inside of you is brighter than the light that's shining on you. When you live for the praise of man, you can be destroyed by the opinion of man. God is looking for people that will be faithful in ALL seasons of development.

"God has already discovered you—He created you. He wants to take us into the darkroom and form His image inside of us in the secret place, where no one can see. If we don't understand this process of development, we will confuse it with missing out. We start to get afraid that what we have to bring will go to waste, and no one will ever appreciate or see it.

We live in a culture where the spotlight is always on us. If the world won't put the spotlight on us, we will put the spotlight on ourselves and upload it to the world. If the spotlight that is on you is greater than the light that is inside of you, it will destroy you."

Caine's talk featured a brilliant analogy, drawing parallels between the premature spotlight and 35mm cameras. Indeed, prior to digital cameras, picture film had to go through darkroom development.

During high school, I enrolled in photography classes where I had the chance to capture and develop my own pictures in a darkroom. It's pitch-black inside—completely impenetrable. Why? Because your film will be ruined if it is exposed to any amount of light, even the smallest glimmer.

Christine Caine then compared this process to us being developed by God. When a believer is being developed in the darkroom, the Father makes sure no spotlight touches him before he is ready for it. He wants to make sure we are ripe for the spotlight. He wants to make sure the spotlight of men will not ruin the gentle light of Christ He has been developing in us—often in the dark, in isolation, and away from the distracting attention of others.

Character: Forged in Fire and Isolation

"Men of genius are admired, men of wealth are envied, men of power are feared, but only men of character are trusted." ~Zig Ziglar

Truthfully, the extent of your character's depth is what determines your quality as a leader of men, or among men. Fostering trust through integrity behavior and practice speaks volumes about you; more than a billion followers ever could.

Furthermore, the best time to develop impeccable character is *before* you ever have followers—in the relative anonymity of your daily walk. It happens best when the spotlight is not yet on you. Yes, it happens in the crucible of the darkroom.

Once you gain followers, it's then time to put that character to the test. And trust me, it will—they will.

Having followers typically leads to increased traction, which can result in more money, fame, or influence. With such influence, you wield more *power*. And the best way to test a man's character is to give him *power*.

Once you have power, it might be too late to work on your character. Remember this while you navigate through this obscure period, diligently improving your leadership skills.

Norman Schwarzkopf, the decorated Desert Storm General, once observed that *"Most leadership failures occur because of a lack of character."*

The character of an individual is formed through virtuous daily personal decisions coupled with intentional self-leadership. It is also fortified through what they value in matters of morals and integrity and how they apply it.

People of prominent character always demand more of themselves than those of poor character. They set the bar higher. It demonstrates their self-worth and their consideration for others. Elevating your personal expectations leads to improved performance in meeting others' expectations. It makes you more trustworthy, competent, and respected. In the end, it gives you a much stronger leadership foundation that establishes itself on trust.

So, if you feel like you have a shortage of followers, the content of your character is the first thing to examine. John Wooden, the famed UCLA basketball coach, said:

"The truest test of a man's character is what he does when no one is watching."

When you're alone in the darkroom, if your character holds up, it will probably pass the subsequent test of public scrutiny.

Nevertheless, keep in mind that even the most skilled leaders have character flaws and can encounter numerous critics along their journey.

Treasures of Darkness

Not everyone realizes this, but darkness isn't entirely negative. Darkness can reveal one-of-a-kind treasures that are hidden from the light.

If you find yourself in a dark place where God feels absent. If you're currently trapped in a dark place where the light cannot penetrate, and everything feels hopeless. If you have lost sight of hope, and you feel like you are beneath the castle of despair, in a dark dungeon; dear reader, chances are that you're being prepared and molded to embrace your purpose as a leader, and perhaps even an extraordinary destiny.

C.S. Lewis, the beloved Christian writer and apologist, said, *"Hardships often prepare ordinary people for an extraordinary destiny."*

Tucked away in the book of Isaiah, there is a verse that is absolutely wonderful. A verse that can provide understanding in times of surrounding darkness. It is found in Isaiah 45:3, where Yahweh says:

"And I will give you treasures hidden in the darkness—secret riches. I will do this so you may know that I am the Lord, the God of Israel, the one who calls you by name." (NLT)

The NIV phrases it this way:

"I will give you hidden treasures, riches stored in secret places, so that you may know that I am the Lord, the God of Israel, who summons you by name."

Treasures hidden in darkness? Hidden treasures?

Through this time of molding, keep in mind, dear leader, that diamonds, gold, and all precious stones are found in the deep and dark recesses of the earth.

But there are more treasures found in darkness.

Consider how human embryos are formed in darkness. If you've ever watched a video showing the accelerated development of a tiny child in the mother's womb, it is absolutely miraculous! And it all happens in darkness.

Likewise, when you feel surrounded by darkness, God is getting ready to birth something amazing within you and through your life! You are, without a doubt, transforming into the leader you are meant to be.

Seeds, when planted, develop in utter darkness. A seed will not sprout unless covered in darkness. In the same way, when you find yourself in darkness, you are being made to sprout, and grow, and bring forth much fruit.

There are also biblical examples of how treasures of darkness brought the best leaders out of obscurity. Consider the preparation of these mighty men of God:

1. Joseph was being prepared to become Prime Minister in Egypt while in a prison dungeon for years—in darkness.

2. The apostle Paul, following his encounter with Christ, was made blind for three days. He was in total darkness—for three whole days. God used this time to download His treasures of darkness in the ex-persecutor of the Church to make him shine the light of Christ. Paul was being prepared, in darkness, for one of the most powerful ministries in the history of the Church!

3. The Bible tells us that Christ got up to go pray while it was still *dark*. In Mark 1:35 we read: *"Rising very early in the morning, <u>while it was still dark</u>, he departed and went out to a desolate place, and there he prayed."* Now there's a powerful picture! Our Lord knew that His Father bestows treasures in darkness! He sought those treasures daily—literally!

4. The most powerful treasure of darkness ever recorded happened while The Son of God was put away *in darkness…* for three days. God then worked his most powerful and earth-shattering treasure of darkness. The resurrection of God's only begotten son was His greatest miracle, which took place while our Lord was in the darkness of the earth.

More Biblical Leaders in the Darkroom

King David, one of history's greatest leaders, often lost hope amidst his many plights. Over and over, he penned his struggles in the Psalms, where he lamented and even despaired of life in a vividly candid fashion.

He didn't write all the Psalms, but there are 42 individual psalms of lament among the 150 psalms—most of them penned by the great king.

The great Protestant Reformer, Martin Luther, treasured the psalms of lament. Of them, he said:

"What is the greatest thing in the Psalter but this earnest speaking amid the storm winds of every kind? [...] Where do you find deeper, more sorrowful, more pitiful words of sadness than in the psalms of lamentation? There again you look into the hearts of the saints, as into death, yes, as into hell itself. When they speak of fear and hope, they use such words that no painter could so depict for your fear or hope, and no Cicero or other orator has so portrayed them. And that they speak these words to God and with God, this I repeat, is the best thing of all. This gives the words double earnestness and life" (Word and Sacrament, Luther's Works, vol. 1, ed. E. T. Bachmann. Philadelphia: Fortress, 1960, pp. 255–56).

The prophet Elijah also found himself in a dark place more than once. In the most notable instance, he had just won a glorious victory against the prophets of Baal, but Jezebel ordered him dead, so he ran—scared for his life. The Bible tells it this way:

"Elijah was afraid and ran for his life. When he came to Beersheba in Judah, he left his servant there, while he himself went a day's journey into the wilderness. He came to a broom bush, sat down under it and prayed that he might die. "I have had enough, Lord," he said. "Take my life; I am no better than my ancestors." ~1 Kings 19:3-4, NIV

The prophet Jonah also had his time in a place of darkness, besides the one in the belly of the great fish, when he also begged for death. So did Job, who, in his darkest time, cursed the day of his birth.

This is to say that even the most exceptional individuals experience discouragement, isolation, and great darkness at some point. At some point, we all find ourselves in a dark place. Maybe you're going through dark times right now. If that's the case, don't lose hope. You're not forgotten. You're not a failure. You're not done. No.

Dear friend, there is good news. You've been planted!

The Humbling of the Darkroom

The story of Joseph in the Old Testament is one of my favorites in Scripture. His incredible journey from despair to success, filled with all the drama, is truly inspiring. But what I like the most about Joseph is his strength of character through it all. He remained steadfast in his faith.

Nevertheless, Joseph wasn't perfect. A subtle clue at the start of his story indicates that Joseph was not particularly humble during his younger years. There was a particular reason why his brothers harbored such strong hatred towards him.

This sibling rivalry can't be entirely blamed on them. I always found that when Joseph had his prophetic dream, he laid it out on the family with an overmeasure of… pride. Don't believe me? Read it for yourself:

"One night Joseph had a dream, and when he told his brothers about it, they hated him more than ever. "Listen to this dream," he said. "We were out in the field, tying up bundles of grain. Suddenly my bundle stood up, and your bundles all gathered around and bowed low before mine!"

His brothers responded, "So you think you will be our king, do you? Do you actually think you will reign over us?" And they hated him all the more because of his dreams and the way he talked about them.

Soon Joseph had another dream, and again he told his brothers about it. "Listen, I have had another dream," he said. "The sun, moon, and eleven stars bowed low before me!"

This time he told the dream to his father as well as to his brothers, but his father scolded him. "What kind of dream is that?" he asked. "Will your mother and I and your brothers actually come and bow to the ground before you?" But while his brothers were jealous of Joseph, his father wondered what the dreams meant." ~Genesis 37:5-11, NLT

Right from the start, Joseph's brothers unmistakably showed their dissatisfaction with his dream. Joseph worsened their animosity by recounting his second dream to them, which involved the sun, moon, and stars also bowing to him. I believe the lad knew exactly what he was doing by sharing his dream;

especially for the second time. In my opinion, he displayed pride and possibly tried to provoke them.

Of course, this doesn't mean he deserved what was to happen to him afterward. He was thrown in a pit by his brothers and then sold as a slave. Later, he was wrongfully accused and thrown in jail. In all, Joseph's darkroom experience took about 13 years—and it was horrendous!

Nevertheless, it worked.

Greatly humbled, he came out of it as one of history's greatest men and leaders.

The Right Heart-itude

Jesus teaches that a disciple is not above his teacher. If He had to go through a period of refinement and preparation (Jesus' so-called lost years, between 12 and 30 years of age), so must we.

This season of preparation in the darkroom is challenging. But, when embraced properly, it can be extremely enriching. Those whose mindset is right for the process can even shorten it. Nevertheless, the season in the darkroom should be approached with great humility and resilience. Believe me, the darkroom will humble those who fail to humble themselves. For no one who is called to leadership can escape its refining fires. So, as they say, you might as well *embrace the suck.*

With this in mind, remember the words of Jesus, who told his disciples: *"Whoever desires to be first among you, let him be your slave."* ~Matthew 20:27, NKJV

I believe that leadership (of people) is something good to aspire to. Nevertheless, as you've probably come to understand so far, I don't believe it is something you must actively seek. Rather, I believe it is something that eventually finds you and that you steadily grow into. It finds you when you have understood that it is not a crown to wear, but a privilege first acquired through competent stewardship. I believe it is an honor that others bestow upon you instead of something that you ever fully deserve. It comes with its fair share of honor, sure, but mostly with a lion's share of responsibility.

This well-known account in the gospel of Matthew expounds perfectly what leadership in the Kingdom should be like:

"Then the mother of Zebedee's sons came to Him with her sons, kneeling down and asking something from Him.

And He said to her, "What do you wish?"

She said to Him, "Grant that these two sons of mine may sit, one on Your right hand and the other on the left, in Your kingdom."

But Jesus answered and said, "You do not know what you ask. Are you able to drink the cup that I am about to drink, and be baptized with the baptism that I am baptized with?"

They said to Him, "We are able."

So He said to them, "You will indeed drink My cup, and be baptized with the baptism that I am baptized with; but to sit on My right hand and on My left is not Mine to give, but it is for those for whom it is prepared by My Father."

*And when the ten heard it, they were greatly displeased with the two brothers. But Jesus called them to Himself and said, "You know that the rulers of the Gentiles lord it over them, and those who are great exercise authority over them. Yet it shall not be so among you; but whoever desires to become great among you, let him be your servant. And whoever desires to be first among you, let him be your slave—just as the Son of Man did not come to be served, but to serve, and to give His life a ransom for many." ~*Matthew 20: 20-28, NKJV

Notice in this passage how Jesus, surprisingly, does *not* rebuke the brother's lofty ambition as something to be scorned. He does, however, take the time to correct their thinking. He says to them, *"Whoever desires to be great among you, let him be your slave."*

But what does that look like, exactly?

The greatest leaders throughout history combined leadership qualities with servant hearts. Their humility prevented them from being self-centered. When we talk about Jesus, Lincoln, or Mother Teresa, we are talking about leaders who espoused great humility.

You see, humble leaders never ask:

- What's in it for *me?*
- Why don't they listen to *me?*
- Why didn't they consider *my idea?*
- Why do they criticize *me?*
- Why don't they recognize *my contributions?*

Most of all, humble leaders don't ask: *Why don't they follow me?*

In the beginning of this book, I shared how troubled I was when I noticed early in my leadership journey that I didn't have any followers. This attitude was one of insecurity, immaturity and, yes, *pride.*

Ego and pride are preoccupied with the absence of followers. Mature leaders, on the other hand, concern themselves with getting their God-given vision to fruition—with or without followers, and no matter the cost. They are concerned about how many people they may help in the process, not with how many people help them or follow them. They are concerned about the progress they make, not about the number of page 'likes' or post 'shares' they get.

Another important distinction is that we are to be slaves (aka servants), sure; *but not servants of people.* Instead, we should be *servants* through a wise usage of our gift, i.e. servants of our gift.

This assertion warrants further clarification.

In our interactions with others, we should have a servant's heart, just like Jesus Christ.

Our gift is the means through which we should serve others. By discovering, developing, and serving our gift, we become its devoted servants. Just as a waiter at a party who serves drinks or appetizers with efficiency and class. We should serve our gift with excellence, enthusiasm, and humility. Every individual should aspire to become a slave… *to his gift!*

I do not wish to be overly blunt, but in this world, most are already slaves to something anyway. Some are slaves to their careers, some to their passions, and some to money or power. All one needs to do is shift his slavish subservience to something honorable, productive, and worthy instead. Our gifts, talents, or abilities certainly qualify, but even more so does Christ, the King. The rightful order of our subservience should then be:

1. Christ first by developing and bettering our talents for His glory.
2. Others seond, by serving it (our gift) to them.

So, yes, become a slave. But be a wise, competent, and useful slave. Avoid becoming an aimless servant of people and their capricious whims.

As Henry David Thoreau said: *"Aim above morality. Be not simply good. Be good for something."*

Humble Yourself or Life Will

Let us then consider the virtue of humility further. Alfred Tennyson, a baron and renowned poet, said of it: *"True humility is the highest virtue, the mother of them all."*

I too believe humility is not only the opposite of pride, but the chief virtue which should accompany the mantle of leadership.

Someone once asked Augustine, the early Church father, what was the first of the religious graces, and he said, *"Humility."* They asked him what was the second, and he replied, *"Humility."* They asked him about the third and he said, *"Humility."*

Indeed, if we are genuinely humble, we will possess numerous other virtues. Many virtues find refuge under the precious umbrella of humility.

Keep in mind also that humility doesn't mean to consider yourself weaker, less intelligent, or less competent than others. Not at all! Humility is a just assessment of one's true strengths, weaknesses, and competencies, and the ability to channel one's strengths potently, or to compensate for one's weaknesses using other's contributions. As C.S. Lewis put it, *"True humility is not thinking less of yourself, it is thinking of yourself less."*

There is a great story of Abraham Lincoln where we see the humility of this U.S. president shine forth:

During the civil war, Lincoln, under severe political pressure, signed an order to transfer certain regiments from one field of battle to another. But Edwin M. Stanton, Lincoln's Secretary of War, refused to carry out the orders.

"Lincoln is a damn fool for ever signing the order," Stanton snorted.

The remark was passed to Lincoln, who did not disagree. "If Stanton said I'm a damn fool, then I must be one," the President replied. "He is nearly always right in military matters. I'll step over and find out what his reasoning is."

Stanton, with a greater understanding of warfare than Lincoln, persuaded his commander-in-chief of the foolishness of the directive. Without delay, Lincoln withdrew it, ultimately saving the lives of thousands of Union troops and averting a disaster.

Lincoln's humility was never a weakness. It was a strength. We often think of leadership as being strong, decisive, bold, and ultra-confident, but if these characteristics are not accompanied by genuine humility, all you have is tyranny.

Make humility a priority and you will lose much concern about having followers.

Make humility a priority and you will become a leader worth following.

Make humility a priority and, chances are, people will honor you and perhaps even follow you.

A Seed Must Die to Fulfill Its Destiny

Earlier I mentioned that if you find yourself in a dark season of seeming endless of painful isolation and fruitlessness, you are far from done. You've likely been planted. The Lord often used agriculture for his metaphors about life and Kingdom living. Speaking of Himself, He mentioned something about seed and how they are meant to bear fruit:

*"Most assuredly, I say to you, unless a grain of wheat falls into the ground and dies, it remains alone; but if it dies, it produces much grain. He who loves his life will lose it, and he who hates his life in this world will keep it for eternal life." ~*John 12:24, NKJV

When a seed dies, it does so in the soil, in utter darkness. It is alone, unseen. Before it can grow into its intended purpose, *it must die.* And it does. Then it sprouts forth with new life and it sheds its former containment shell. Finally, it grows from root, to shoot, to mature plant, to fruit.

And so it is with impactful men and women who are called to add to the world. It is necessary for you to be well-versed in this process. Embrace it, and understand that treasures of darkness can be unearthed. Ironically, these treasures of darkness will bring much light. But, yes, this progression usually involves a form of death—a death to self. Whether it is a death to self, or to your ambition, or to your family, of to your lofty dreams—you leave behind something of your former self and thus emerge transformed. So, while it is true that *what doesn't kill you makes you stronger*, it is only this inner death to self that can make you fruitful and perhaps even transcend mortality.

Sometimes, the process of the seed dying may seem to be depressingly interminable. Such is the case with…

The Bamboo Tree

Les Brown, a well-known motivational speaker and author, once shared an illustration that went something like this:

A Chinese bamboo tree takes five years to grow. It has to be watered and fertilized in the ground where it has been planted every day. It doesn't break through the ground for *five years*. There it remains, hidden, under the soil, in complete darkness. The ignorant may give up on it, thinking the seed never sprouted—that it died.

But… after five years, a miracle of nature takes place. The seed finally sprouts and breaks through.

And once it breaks through the ground, it will grow 90 feet tall in five weeks! Up to two feet a day! Now, the question is: did the Chinese bamboo tree grow 90 feet tall in five weeks, or in five years? According to Brown, the answer is obvious; it grows 90 feet tall in 5 years. If at any time that person stopped watering and fertilizing that tree, it would just die in the ground.

You too, dear leader, will at times feel like nothing is happening during your "dark night of the soul". And yet, this period spent in the wilderness, in the blackness of the darkroom; this time under the soil after you've been planted, will most likely make you grow and mature more than any amount of success ever would.

It did for me.

The Unique Challenge of Rest

When you find yourself in the crucible of the darkroom, you inevitably find yourself invited to a season of rest. Leaders are often wired as the doers of the world. Therefore, as a leader, resting and waiting patiently to renew your strength can prove challenging. As you traverse the darkroom's eerie stillness and apparent abandonment, your own existence may come into question. You must avoid this trap.

The book of Ecclesiastes (chapter 3) reminds us that there is a time for everything, and that for every season, there is a reason. There is, for sure, a time to work, and a time to rest.

Sometimes you will find yourself in a season where *massive action* is your prime directive and a required course. At such times, there's no *if's* or *but's* about it—you just know what you've got to do, and you feel like there's a fire under you pushing you to do it. You know you have to *do it now*. During those times, even though you may feel overwhelmed and on the verge of losing your mind, you find a way to overcome, right?

The hustle makes sense to us as it propels us forward, but the silence of life often confounds us when nothing seems to happen. And yet, these are the times we learn the most about God, ourselves, and our very lives. The darkroom is an unheralded time of inner and unseen productivity. It is a time when we enrich ourselves inwardly through some much-needed soul-searching. It is often the best time for a life-altering encounter with the light of Jesus Christ.

A leader who finds himself in the darkroom's crucible must often be reminded to *be still, and know that He is God* (Psalm 46:10)—and that he, despite his often-pretentious posing, is not.

So, if you are presently being developed in the darkroom, my advice is to embrace the process and all of its complex simplicity. Use it as a time of deep reflection and prayer, but also as a time of thanksgiving for what God is about to burst forth through you.

I dare you… ask Him to birth great things through you. You'll marvel at the power and results that may follow such a petition.

The Agony of the Cross Before

During His life and ministry, the Lord faced many instances where He found Himself alone in the darkroom, developing His marvellous gift. Toward the end of His earthly life, some of the most notable instances were…

- Anguishing in Gethsemane.
- Abandoned while hanging on the cross. And, of course…
- Three days and nights visiting death and Hades in the belly of the earth.

If there's anything we can learn from the life and death of Christ, it's that before any great leader makes it to glory, there has to be a process—most often painful, lonely, and dark, where he can literally go through hell.

Most leaders who have a high calling must be willing to embrace the agony of the cross before they can savor the glory of the resurrection. Thus, the pain of their sanctification births the impact of their significance.

Sam Chand, Author of 'Leadership Pain,' rightly observed: *"The difference between where you are and where God wants you to be is the pain you are unwilling to endure."*

Bible teacher A. W. Tozer put it this way:

"It is doubtful whether God can bless a man greatly until he has hurt him deeply."

Cradles of Eminence

I have an interesting book at home titled: *Cradles of Eminence: Childhoods of More Than 700 Famous Men and Women*. It was penned by Victor Goertzel, with his own family helping with the research involved. While it is a book, it reads more like a doctoral research paper. The thesis of the book, however, is fairly straightforward and very powerful. Essentially, it delves into the idea that many successful individuals in various fields had a troubled or dysfunctional childhood. In other words, they had to undergo growing pains and seasons of darkness in their youth.

In his research, Goertzel states how these eminent adults in their childhoods often share the following backgrounds:

- They strongly disliked school, struggling throughout, but had families who valued education.
- They often had a dysfunctional, failure-prone father.
- They had highly opinionated parents, often with a dominating mother.
- They grew up "feeling different" from others, and were often alone, isolated, even ostracized.

What do we then learn from these famous and successful people, these *Leaders?* Simply that they could not avoid the required toll that was to lead them toward success and recognition. The disagreeable fact is that nobody can.

In the most recent edition of *Cradles of Eminence,* readers are challenged to consider what factors will foster eminence in today's world of mass media and technological change. I address this very question in later chapters of this book.

Be Patient with Yourself

Typically, a leader's lack of followers is because of being in the start-up phase, as we have seen. No matter how strong your character, how much service you offer, or how humble you are, it doesn't matter. When you begin your purpose-related work and life-calling, chances are you will have very few followers at first. Depending on many other key factors (location, visibility, calling, marketing, people skills, affluence) you may remain without followers anywhere from a few days, to a few weeks, to a few years. And let's be brutally honest here; for some, success may never happen. I will address this possibility in more detail later.

For now, however, the question you have to ask yourself is this… *Are you able to live with this prospect?*

Are your vision and goals strong enough to sustain you through years of doing it alone? Celebrated author Ernest Hemingway once remarked:

"You must be prepared to work always without applause."

You see, this desert phase of the budding leader is the truest test of his mettle. It is a test of his character and commitment. The true leader with a genuine vision will remain undaunted by a lack of followers or recognition. In fact, the stronger leaders are those who remain true to their purpose in the long run, regardless of how many people bought into it as well.

Trust the God Behind the Process

The work God is doing during this dark time is molding treasures of darkness within you. The light is not where these treasures can be discovered or cultivated. They can only be bestowed to you in dark times—during what some have called *the dark night of the soul*—in the darkroom.

When faced with darkness, our hunger for enlightenment makes us more receptive. We are hungrier for the light of His truth—Son-light. We are more sensitive to the light of His correction.

In darkness, He can provide us with treasures that are unique to these moments. These *treasures of darkness* will be the most precious ones you carry. So, dear leader, keep in mind God wants to use these and turn…

Your mess into a message

Your misery into a ministry

Your pain into a platform

Your test into a testimony

Your lack into a legacy

Your chaos into a crown.

And always remember…

"The darkest nights produce the brightest stars." ~John Greene

"It's always darkest before the dawn." ~Thomas Fuller

So, hang in there, dear leader, for *this too shall pass.*

CHAPTER 4

Autopsy of a Follower

"The object of life is not to be on the side of the majority, but to escape finding oneself in the ranks of the insane."

~Marcus Aurelius

A blog I read recently highlighted the large quantities of headless ancient Roman sculptures. The article's objective was to elucidate this phenomenon. Among the erroneous theories discussed are mishandling during transport or the idea that the decapitations are just a result of normal wear and tear. The actual explanation, which is quite fascinating, expounded on how the Romans went to the trouble of commissioning statues specifically designed with detachable heads. The reason they did is even more interesting. The idea was that if the selected personality to be made into a statue loses fame, honor, or dies, their head can be quickly swapped with someone else's. The sculptures in these instances featured a generic body and interchangeable heads, lacking any specific identity. According to Ancient Roman culture, a person's identity was largely associated with their head and face, not their body.

Expert historians have extensively documented this societal practice. According to Thomas Dudley Fosbroke's writings in the *Encyclopaedia of Antiquities and Elements of Archaeology (Volume 1, "Greek Sculpture," p. 137)*:

"It being usual upon many occasions to put other heads upon statues, Caesar took off that of the Alexander of Lysippus, and substituted his own. This was commonly done with regard to deposed Emperors."

So, the detachable heads of the Roman statues symbolize not only the ephemeral nature of worldly leaders but also people's fickleness as followers. Roman society chose leaders they admired and immortalized them as statues, but swiftly replaced their heads if they grew displeased.

One of their own poets said it best:

"The fickle populace always changes with the prince." ~Claudius Claudianus

Defining Followers

It is often said that people in the world can be divided into two groups: *Leaders* and *Followers*.

But here's what I discovered: People dislike seeing themselves as followers, and in general, they don't want to be leaders either. Assuming otherwise is a mistake.

Even though they require leaders, individuals desire the freedom to choose who they follow and when, while also believing they are in control. Also, generally speaking, they try to avoid the burden of leadership. Conversely, they certainly do not like to be portrayed or thought of as followers. Well, for this at least, I can't really blame them. The dictionary definition of follower isn't very flattering.

follower: /ˈfälōər/noun, 1. adherent, partisan; refers to someone who shows allegiance to a person, a doctrine, a cause, and the like. Follower often has an implication of personal relationship or of *slavish acquiescence*. 2. a person who moves or travels behind someone or something.

That last part of the first definition, the... *slavish acquiescence*. Yeah, that one hurts. Right? And the other one, stating how followers find themselves behind someone or something. That sucks too. That's the stigma associated with the word 'follower'. That's why people generally don't like to consider themselves *followers*. And yet, ironically, few people consider themselves *strong leaders* either. But the fact remains that most individuals tend to follow rather than lead. The majority of individuals lack the steadfast self-discipline required for *personal leadership* (see 'Terms of Contention' in chapter 1). Sadly, only a few individuals uncover their talents and develop them purposefully. An even smaller percentage possess the authentic desire and ability to lead and make a positive impact on others.

Why is that? You ask.

Well, to be blunt, because following is less demanding less than leading. It's like the old saying, *"Everyone wants to go to heaven, but nobody wants to die."* We could paraphrase it this way when it comes to leadership:

"Everyone wants to be regarded as a leader, but nobody wants to lead."

The Follower's 'WHY?'

"Folly is wont to have more followers and comrades than discretion." ~Miguel Cervantes

Why would Miguel Cervantes, the famous Spanish author of *Don Quixote,* assert such a thing? Well, clearly, the man understood that followers can be quite demanding and fickle. Their feelings towards you can change astonishingly fast, whether it's due to your words, actions, or lack thereof.

Some will be loyal for years and suddenly stop following you for no apparent reason. Others are all about perks, promotions, or freebies, and will stop following as soon as the promise of those ceases.

In all honesty, I am no exception. For instance, I used to follow a certain Christian ministry because I loved getting their free books or other trinkets. But one day, when I received another letter inviting me to give to their ministry, I felt deeply convicted. I was only a taker and had been for years. So, I didn't renew my subscription to their mailing list for matters of conscience.

The truth is that followers, unlike leaders, always have a *'What's in it for me?'* mentality. Most people, even those with good intentions, ultimately follow leaders for their own benefit. It's normal, expected, and we all do it to some extent. So, we can't hold it against anyone.

For instance, even individuals aspiring to learn from the leader on how to serve others better (a noble intention) are driven by selfish motives.; i.e. *"I need this knowledge to better myself."*

In an excellent article titled *7 Reasons Why Followers Follow*, Jack Dunigan explores the main motives of followers. He listed the following:

1. **The anticipation of discovery**. The possibility of new things attracts people, especially when there's a promise of reward.

2. **The prospect of a better life**. The desire to better one's status is nearly universal.

3. **The possibility of greater good**. The idea of making a significant positive impact on others is appealing to many.

4. **The relief from great discomfort.** Certain individuals feel the need to escape due to their present conditions.

5. **The expectation of fulfilled hope**. Ideals look for expression. Some followers are drawn to leaders who pledge to fulfill their long-held aspirations. Typically, it falls into the categories of political, charitable, religious, or a blend of them all.

6. **The expression of practical values**. When values come together, they form a powerful dynamic.

7. **The protection of tangible and intangible assets**. For instance, in order to safeguard their families and countries, soldiers willingly take on great risks. On a less vivid scale, employees are motivated to follow company leaders by the promise of preserving their existing assets and gaining additional benefits.

Read the full article here: http://thepracticalleader.com/7-reasons-why-followers-follow/

With the exception of the third reason (The possibility of greater good), the motives of followers are, sadly, selfish or self-centered to some degree. In saying this, I am not condemning followers, for I too am one. I am merely pointing out the base motivations of followers—which, again, are only human.

We examined in chapter 1 how the Lord Jesus Christ understood that many who followed Him did so because he provided bread. They liked the free meals. He knew it and even confronted them about it (John 6:26). Understanding the tendency of followers to be self-centered is essential for effective leadership, regardless of your current follower status.

The whole idea behind leadership is to *lead*. A leader cannot entertain the same motives as a follower. He must march to the beat of a different drummer. He must elevate his way of thinking. As a leader, you must understand that those who lead best are those who serve best. So, while followers may be naturally selfish and seek what's in it for them, it is the responsibility of the leader to be *unselfish*.

This is how leaders separate themselves from followers. This is how leaders show the way.

What Followers Provide

Being a leader doesn't require having followers, but I want to make sure I'm not misunderstood throughout the book. I wouldn't invalidate the many *positive aspects* of a strong followership or of meaningful connections for any leader. After all, success, in all of its forms, is tied to people-dynamics. It always has been and always will be. It comes through people's appreciation, validation, and endorsement of your message, product, or service. That's an inescapable fact. So, while failure to gather followers doesn't diminish your worth, it does diminish your net worth.

After all, followers can help a leader to…

- Gain access to more opportunities
- Grow his circle of influence
- Sell basically anything
- Receive recognition and/or promotions
- Reproduce himself (impart knowledge, skill, or wisdom)
- Receive feedback (whether positive or negative)
- Work with a team or in a partnership, thus lessening his burden

For any leader, these are all *positive things*. Especially if your endeavors add value to people and are honorable. So, for sure, if a larger followership presents itself to you, receive it with gratitude—and run with the people spearheading you. Never forget that as a leader, it is an honor to be followed, even if just by one person. While we should never force or coerce individuals to follow, we should gratefully welcome them on our journey.

- You don't need followers to be a leader, *but you need followers to make an impact.*

- You don't need followers to be a leader, *but you need people to make meaningful connections and build a team.*

- You don't need followers to be a leader, *but you need others to get a break or an opportunity.*

- You don't need followers to be a leader, *but you need followers to be successful.*

Conversely, though, having a substantial following, particularly in great numbers, can also pose its own challenges. A considerable number of followers can cause a leader to prioritize fickle demands, potentially diverting a more easily influenced leader from his primary mission or tasks. So, be advised that the good also comes with the bad. While the advantages are undeniable, more followers also mean more demands and more criticism. This may or may not be something that works for you. Therefore, it would be wise to ask yourself the following question…

Are You Seeking Followers or Validation?

I urge you to probe your own motives. While it is acceptable for entrepreneurs or business leaders to wish for more customers, who may later turn into raving fans for a product or service, you must avoid the trap of seeking followers to feel validated. As a leader, you must first seek to be efficient in your calling and purpose. This is your priority. Seeking more followers can divert you from your true mission and likely turn you into a *people pleaser*.

What happens when you become a people pleaser? From a Kingdom perspective—*not much*. Nevertheless, I must distinguish between people-pleasing and wanting to serve people or adding value to them.

- When you serve people, you aim to help them. When you please people, you aim to help yourself.

- When you serve people, you want to make sure they're all right. When you please people, you want to make sure they think you're all right.

- When you serve people, you want to see them grow. When you please people, you want to see yourself grow.

- When you serve people, you want to please God. When you please people, you want to please men.

When trying to please people rather than serve them, you ever so subtly shift from being purpose-centered and God-focused to being man-focused.

Let's face it, when you become overly concerned with followers and people's desires or opinions, you are acting more out of fear than out of faith. In essence, you're transitioning from considering God's thoughts to considering men's thoughts. And the Bible tells us very succinctly that *the fear of man is a snare* (Proverbs 29:25).

David's Census

While scholars may disagree on *who* prompted King David to conduct a census of Israel's troops in the Bible (God himself—2 Samuel 24, or Satan—1 Chronicles 21), one thing is certain: it was a sin which greatly displeased the Lord and slowly led the great king down the wrong moral path, ultimately leading to his adultery with Bathsheba.

But why did this census anger Yahweh? What was it *exactly* that was wrong for King David to number his troops?

Simply put, it showed how David's heart was being led astray.

This census was an outward manifestation of where David's trust was now shifting toward. In short, his focus shifted from the greatness of his God to the greatness of his army. He trusted in the might of his troops more than Almighty God's hand.

This attitude angered Yahweh. And while David repented, he still had to endure the consequence of his sin. The Israelites suffered a great and deadly plague, which led the king to plead with God, praying:

"Was it not I who ordered the fighting men to be counted? I, the shepherd, have sinned and done wrong. These are but sheep. What have they done? Lord my God, let your hand fall on me and my

family, but do not let this plague remain on your people." ~1 Chronicles 21:17, NIV

Despite the king's sincere repentance and strong leadership disposition, God did not heed his plea. As a result, the numbers in Israel were greatly decimated. 70,000 people died of this plague. This seemingly harsh punishment nonetheless fit the crime. God took away the crutch David relied on: strong numbers of people.

But, deep down, we're not any better, are we?

We too, at times, rely more on man than we do on the Lord. We too, as leaders, often place too high a value on the number of our followers—whether they are online, at work, or in ministry, to measure our worth and success.

I, for one, admit that I've gotten a jolt of satisfaction at times when I would consider my number of views on YouTube, or my positive book reviews on Amazon. But this belies a deeper problem.

If we number our followers regularly, this is a clear indication that we are insecure. This clearly shows that we rely on people instead of God and the journey we're on. We place a numerical value on our worth, but numbers, as we have seen, hold little significance in God's economy. Evidently, the Father is more concerned with the content of our character than with the height of our achievements.

Moreover, relying on your follower count is an inadequate way to gauge your true worth.

The Leadership Lid and Its Bias

In his seminal leadership book, *The 21 Irrefutable Laws of Leadership*, John C. Maxwell introduced *the law of the lid* as the first of the 21 laws. The law of the lid is described this way:

"Leadership ability is the lid that determines a person's level of effectiveness. The lower an individual's ability to lead, the lower the lid on his potential. The higher the individual's ability to lead, the higher the lid on his potential. To give you an example, if your leadership rates an 8, then your effectiveness can never be greater than a 7. If your leadership is only a 4, then your effectiveness will be no higher than a 3. Your leadership ability—for better or for worse—always determines your effectiveness and the potential impact of your organization."

So, the general rule is that only those under you in leadership ability will follow you. That is what can be called *a person's true leadership lid*. Leaders with a leadership lid rating of 7/10 will generally only draw in followers who score 6 or less.

But, to every rule, there are exceptions.

Our human nature is the root of the problem, as we tend to view ourselves as the center of the universe and make judgments based on that perspective.

When discussing the concept of the leadership lid, there is a noticeable phenomenon associated with this law. Let's call it *'the perceived leadership lid'* or *'the leadership lid bias'*.

The *perceived leadership lid* puts a damper on *the law of the lid*. It creates a dreaded 'exception to the rule'.

So, let's examine how this affects you and your potential followers.

First, let's examine your follower's own perceived leadership lid.

As you know, everyone has an opinion of themselves. Generally, this opinion is accompanied by serious blind spots. Depending on the individual, some see themselves as better than they really are, and others see themselves as worse than they really are.

Your genuine leadership lid, then, is subject to the self-perception of your follower's own perceived leadership lid.

What does this mean?

Well, if any of your follower's self-perceived lid is higher than your real or perceived leadership lid, *they will not follow you.* For instance, if your potential follower perceives himself as having a leadership lid (ability) of 8, when they are in reality a 5, they will not follow you—even if you are a 7. Why? Because they see themselves as a better leader than you. Period. That is their biased, or perceived, leadership lid. So, are they wrong? Sure. But regardless of their error, the fact remains: they are not your follower. Despite your genuine ability to guide them towards greater heights, understanding, or achievement, they remain oblivious.

Keep in mind, also, that most of us are vulnerable to this error in judgment. We are all prone to biased self-awareness.

The flip side of the coin is the follower's flawed perception of *your* leadership lid.

While your potential follower may have an adequate grasp of their own leadership lid, this doesn't guarantee they have adequate judgement of your leadership lid.

For example, if your potential follower sees himself as a 6, and is indeed a 6 in reality; this doesn't guarantee they will follow a 7. Why is that? Simply because losing a follower is possible if they see you as a 5 instead of your true 7. A 6 will never follow a perceived 5; even if that perceived 5 is in fact a 7.

Do you understand these principles? Good, because I would hate to go through that explanation again. I'm exhausted just re-reading it!

But all joking aside, what does this all mean? That some people might be below you in terms of leadership capacity or ability, but will never follow you because, pridefully or erroneously, they see themselves as superior to you, or they see you as inferior to them. That bias is what I coined *the leadership lid bias*.

Ultimately, nobody will ever follow a leader they feel is inferior to them. Followership is that subjective. Period. The apostle Paul understood this bias when he penned these words in his second epistle to the Corinthians:

"You are judging by appearances. If anyone is confident that they belong to Christ, they should consider again that we belong to Christ just as much as they do. So even if I boast somewhat freely about the authority the Lord gave us for building you up rather than tearing you down, I will not be ashamed of it. I do not want to seem to be trying to frighten you with my letters. For some say, "His letters are weighty and forceful, but in person he is unimpressive and his speaking

amounts to nothing." Such people should realize that what we are in our letters when we are absent, we will be in our actions when we are present." ~2 Corinthians 10:7-11, (NIV)

Your Perceived Value vs. Your Real Value

"Success is not the crown of leadership; for the law decrees that failure may crown the greatest effort." ~The Kolbrin, Book of Morals and Precepts.

Know this: a leader's followership is *always* determined by his *perceived value* and contribution, and not necessarily by his real value and contribution. Again, we tend to *perceive* a leader's followership as a sign of his worthiness. We see it as a sign of his quality as a person or leader.

And yet, in the Bible, what did Jesus say to those who wouldn't follow Him unless He proved Himself with a sign? In Matthew 16:1-4, we read:

"The Pharisees and Sadducees came to Jesus and tested him by asking him to show them a sign from heaven. He replied, "When evening comes, you say, 'It will be fair weather, for the sky is red,' and in the morning, 'Today it will be stormy, for the sky is red and overcast.' You know how to interpret the appearance of the sky, but you cannot interpret the signs of the times. A wicked and adulterous generation looks for a sign, but none will be given it except the sign of Jonah." Jesus then left them and went away."

This is how any of us should deal with lack of followership nowadays. Just like Jesus, you also have a mission to complete. And like Him, you should not waste your time. The Lord didn't have time to indulge those who didn't see or understand His value. He knew His worth, and that was sufficient. These people weren't worth His time or effort, and so *'He left them and went away.'*

We should always leave those types of people behind, even if we have no followers to speak of. Those are not people you want following you. Or, as business jargon would put it, they are not your tribe. Their minds are made up about you. Why exert yourself to change it and become their slave in the process?

Take the example of Noah. His *perceived value* was extremely low. He had gathered no followers. Most of his contemporaries thought him insane to be building a ship in a mostly deserted place. In reality, though, his real value was very high. So much so, in fact, that those who would've followed him would have been contributors to humanity's future in no small way.

Conversely, let's consider certain social media sensations. For instance, some girls on social media have an immense followership (in the millions) because they dress provocatively and use their sex-appeal to sell a product or gain a substantial followership and make money.

In such cases, the *perceived value* is, unfortunately, high. But in reality, the true value is low. The obvious reason being that this is not a service or skill that can bring humanity much higher in terms of advancement, knowledge, health, survival, character, or industriousness—quite the opposite. Nor will these individuals impact history in any significant way. So, in the realm of genuine value and sustainability, in the grand scheme of things, it is *highly insignificant*. We must, therefore, keep these things in perspective as we consider the value people bring.

When comparing star athletes and doctors, the same assertion can be made. What is the rationale behind the salary difference between an NBA star earning $10 million per year and a family doctor earning approximately $250,000? This defies logic because both fall under the 'perceived value' bias of society.

Perceived value is thus determined by the following:

- Environment
- Trends
- Relatability
- Need
- Influence

If, for example, you were to consider the biggest social media influencers of our current era, you would probably reach the sad conclusion that, for the most part, their contribution to the betterment of humanity is quite low. This is a reflection of how the above bulleted list is scaled in our evaluations. It is also a reflection of our own failing system of values and morals as a society.

Rest assured, we'll dive in *much deeper* into social media influence in later chapters.

Why Your Helpers Won't Follow You

I would now like to address the different types of people you will connect with, and why they may or may not follow your leadership.

Even if you become an outstanding leader, it is unlikely that past acquaintances who share the same lane of expertise and who helped or supported you will become your followers. I mean, here, individuals who are in the same business, profession, or lane as you. This, too, has to do with *the leadership lid bias.*

I have observed this time and again in my own life. It doesn't matter what you go on to accomplish after these individuals help you. It doesn't matter if you go on to become president or CEO of a mega-corporation, a world-renowned genius, or even a multi-millionaire. If they previously were in a position where they helped you up the mountain, that settles it. In their mind, their lid is higher than yours. It is established, cast in concrete. Therefore, do not be shocked when those who previously helped you show little or no interest in your subsequent accomplishments.

This is just the way of human nature and its dynamics — most of the time, anyway.

Why Family Members Won't Follow You

There is an interesting account in the life of Christ that is seldom taught. It is the following:

"While he was still speaking to the people, behold, his mother and his brothers stood outside, asking to speak to him. But he replied to the man who told him, "Who is my mother, and who are my brothers?" And stretching out his hand toward his disciples, he said, "Here are my mother and my brothers! For whoever does the will of my Father in heaven is my brother and sister and mother." ~Matthew 12:46-50, ESV

And, in the gospel of Mark, we read:

"Then he went home, and the crowd gathered again, so that they could not even eat. And when his family heard it, they went out to seize him, for they were saying, "He is out of his mind." ~Mark 3:20-21, ESV

When you embrace the spirit of leadership and pursue your calling wholeheartedly, it's likely that even your family will question your worth, and perhaps even your sanity. If it happened to the Lord, it's within the realm of possibility for us as well.

"But why?" you ask?

Well, most times, these people grew up with you or raised you. They've seen you at your best, but also at your worse, warts and all. Their reasoning is simple: why should *you* rise above them or be esteemed differently?

It can be tough for relatives to acknowledge someone's success if they have similar genetic origins, as it brings to light their own unachieved dreams, setbacks, and untapped abilities. Your success both encourages them to strive for more while also implying they are not doing enough.

I've seen it many times. When I coach authors, many of them lament the fact that their own family members don't read the books they've written.

I've also heard stories from well-known experts, motivational speakers, or life coaches who have faced disbelief and rejection from their own families.

When it comes to my own family, I can attest to the same in various respects. To my knowledge, my sibling, uncles, aunts, and cousins haven't made any effort to read my works or listen to my teachings. Unless, of course, there's a chance they could be…

Covert Followers

When a man or woman stands out among their peers through sheer will, potential, and innovative thinking, although they may not always have followers, they never seem to be without *covert followers*.

I found this to be true of myself, but also of others. And, in all honesty I, at times, have found myself as a secret follower of a select few for varying reasons. I'm sure you have, too.

Covert followers are either:

- Those too shy to follow you openly.
- Those who are just curious as to what you are doing.
- Those who might have helped you in the past who wish to remain anonymous.
- Those who are envious, and wish to see you fail miserably.

Covert followers are a fascinating breed. They can range from harmless to good or even bad. Certain individuals may begin with curiosity and transform into devoted followers. And some others can become envious and vicious haters later on because of something you did or said.

Of course, in the age of social media, being a covert follower has never been easier. Just click *like*, *follow*, *subscribe*, or *add as friend*, and *voilà*—you can now see what the other person is up to on your phone, tablet, or PC.

It wasn't always so accessible to become a covert follower, however. Back in the olden days, one could only do so cleverly, through stealth.

Here is an interesting example.

Stephen Grellet worked as a missionary during the pioneer era of the United States. He served as a Quaker evangelist, preacher, and missionary. He found himself on the western fringes of the nation, nestled at the base of the Rockies, deep in prayer and communion with God. In that sacred moment, he sensed an inner prompting—that God was urging him to journey to a specific lumber camp and deliver the gospel message. Without hesitation, he obeyed the call, making his way to the designated lumber camp with the anticipation of leading a revival crusade.

When he arrived there, however, there was not a soul in the lumber camp, not one. He looked around and thought; maybe they are over in the mess hall. Stephen Grellet then went over to the mess hall and again, no one was there. So, he prayed, *"Lord, you've told me to come here and preach. I don't understand it, but I'm going to be obedient."*

So, he stood in that empty mess hall and nonetheless preached his heart out. He preached Jesus, salvation, and pled for souls to be saved to an empty place. He gave an invitation for people to receive Christ, then had a benediction, and finally went his way, satisfied that he had been obedient, yet not understanding it at all.

Several years later, on the London Bridge, across the ocean, Stephen Grellet found himself approached by a stranger whose heavy hand landed on his shoulder. The man inquired, *"Are you Stephen Grellet?"* to which he affirmed, *"I am."*

The stranger then revealed, *"I've been searching the world over for you. Do you recall visiting a particular lumber camp at the base of the Rockies and delivering a sermon to an empty mess hall? You might have thought no one heard you, but I did. I served as the foreman of my crew, working in the woods cutting trees, and I had to return for another axe. That's when I overheard you preaching. I stood behind a stack of wood, hesitant to reveal myself, but your words penetrated my heart and stirred conviction within me. I went back into the woods and surrendered my heart to Jesus Christ. I shared the experience with three other lumberjacks, and astonishingly, all three of them also committed their lives to Jesus Christ. Sir, I want you to know that the four of us have since become missionaries and evangelists, fervently spreading the gospel of Jesus Christ."*

Here was a man, Stephen Grellet, obedient to his calling, not knowing why, regardless of any audience or followers, but simply obedient to the call on his life.

A similar lesson is taught in another story as well.

Robert Moffat, a Scottish missionary in South Africa, returned to recruit helpers in Scotland. During one evening, his spirits sank when he discovered that the attendees of his meeting were exclusively women, while his chosen verse, Proverbs 8:4, emphasized *"Unto you, O men, I call."*

So consumed by his bewilderment, he almost overlooked the small boy in the loft, diligently working the bellows of the organ. Realizing the challenging conditions in the undeveloped jungles, Dr. Moffat felt hopeless while conveying the message, aware that only a few women would be willing to endure such rigorous experiences, especially in those days. But God works in mysterious ways to carry out His wise purposes. Although no one volunteered, the young fellow working the organ was deeply challenged. He decided to emulate the pioneer missionary, pursued education, earned a medical degree, and dedicated his life to ministering to Africa's unreached tribes. His name was… David Livingstone. Today, David Livingstone is considered the most renowned missionary ever to set foot in Africa.

So, what is the moral of these two similar accounts? Well, it's pretty simple, really. Whether you have thousands of followers, or seemingly none at all, do what it is you are called to do. And do it well. Because you never know who might be watching from the shadows. You never know who you might impact by your message, courage, or example.

Your Secret (and Not-So-Secret) Haters

No impactful figure has been without their fair share of haters. As you embark on your personal journey, chase your passions, and aim to create a positive influence, facing critics is unavoidable. Leaders, especially, require a resilient spirit to withstand the disapproval of the crowd.

A thick skin, therefore, is just one of the many qualities essential for persevering when the murmurs of dissent surround you. It's crucial to acknowledge that your unique talents may not resonate with everyone, and the outspoken crowd will consistently remind you of this reality. Despite the challenge this presents, it is essential to nurture a disregard for what others think or say. Your devotion to your gift, purpose, and God's calling should be so profound that the judgments of others become inconsequential.

James Cook, the British ship captain and cartographer, aptly noted:

"The man who wants to lead the orchestra has to turn his back on the crowd."

Embracing this wisdom means being prepared for whispers behind your back as you forge ahead. Let them talk and carry on. Understand that this is an inherent aspect of the leadership journey. The truth, dear friend, is that you had a purpose before anyone had an opinion. So, ignore the haters, press on, and finish your mission.

Who Do You Follow?

Mostly in our lives, we find ourselves playing the role of a follower rather than a leader. With that in mind, the question is: *Who do you follow? And why?*

Within this double-sided question is the essence of self-awareness and the recognition of the influential forces that shape all of us. The choices we make in terms of individuals, ideologies, and societal trends mold our very lives. So, consider the impact—both positive and negative—that your chosen influences exert upon you. Are the ones you follow leading you towards growth, empathy, and truth, or are they unintentionally steering you towards misguided intentions, falsehood, superficiality, and aimless pursuits?

While we don't have too much control over who chooses to follow us, we have complete control over who we choose to follow.

Dear leader, the decision you make in this matter can profoundly shape your leadership journey. The reason being: we emulate those we look up to, whether we realize it or not.

CHAPTER 5

History's Leaders Without Followers

"A great fire burns within me, but no one stops to warm themselves at it, and passers-by only see a wisp of smoke."

~Vincent Van Gogh

In this chapter, I aim to share with you the biographies of leaders who made groundbreaking advancements or had revolutionary ideas but failed to gather any followers. I'm referring to Leaders Without Followers (LWF's). Just like you and me, they also had to endure the pain of loneliness from time to time. Similar to us, they too might have wished at some point to have people to influence or assist.

Despite their limited following, these leaders excelled in their respective domains. As a result, they should have received a greater sphere of influence and recognition. Sadly, however, in most cases, their following began growing only after their demise.

Nevertheless, I hope these stories will encourage you and uplift you—offering inspiration for the journey. I hope their stories help you stop belittling yourself and realize that even without a huge following, you're in good company.

Noah, 2900 BC

In Genesis chapters 6 through 9 of the Bible, you can find the story of Noah. It's safe to assume you are already familiar with it.

Noah was a just man who *"walked with God"*, amidst a generation that was utterly perverted and corrupt—not just morally, but genetically as well. Therefore, if he was out to attract any followers, the odds were stacked against him from the get-go. Of course, his lack of influence only worsened when God spoke to him and said:

"The end of all flesh has come before Me, for the earth is filled with violence through them; and behold, I will destroy them with the earth. Make yourself an ark of gopherwood; make rooms in the ark, and cover it inside and outside with pitch." ~Genesis 6: 13-14

Despite his efforts, Noah couldn't gather any followers during the ark's construction. No one approached him and said, *"Hey Noah, I want to be a part of this unique project you're working on."*

But this didn't deter Noah.

He had no followers, save for his family; but he clearly wasn't "just talking a walk." And when the time came, he boarded the ark with his wife, three sons, and their respective wives, and the rest, as we know, is history.

There's an interesting meme on social media that wisely observes: *"Everyone thought Noah was crazy, until it started to rain."*

But one question remains, though. Do animals count as followers?

Joseph, 1914 BC to 1804 BC

If you've been to Sunday school, you're probably familiar with the happy ending of Joseph's story. Due to his exceptional skills in dream interpretation, wisdom, and administration, he was chosen as Prime Minister of Egypt in a time of crisis after a challenging season in the darkroom. In addition, he was able to reconcile with his estranged family. Joseph had a vision of this happening when he was young, but he probably didn't foresee it taking place so much later in his life. The Bible tells us, *"Joseph was thirty years old when he stood before Pharaoh, king of Egypt."* ~Genesis 41:46, KJV

He was given a dream of his mighty destiny at the tender age of 17. When his brothers came to Egypt, he had been in power for ten years by that time—he was around 40. Do the math. This means that it took 23 years for Joseph's dream of ruling over his brothers to come true.

From the pit, to slave, to prison, to Prime Minister; Joseph spent 13 years as a leader without followers. Sure, the story has a happy ending, but it's due in large part to his faith and perseverance—while he had little to no recognition from his peers.

Jeremiah, 627-586 BC

Jeremiah is one of the most prominent prophets in the Scriptures. And yet, Jeremiah lived and prophesied at the end of an age. For forty years he had to proclaim a very unpopular warning, which went something like: *'This world, this Kingdom, this comfortable system of life is coming to an end!'*

From a human standpoint, Jeremiah's ministry was an *abject failure.*

Just think about it. For forty years, the Lord had made an impassioned appeal through His prophet, seemingly to no avail. The point was reached when there was no remedy, no healing. The people, from the king to the princes, priests, and commoners; all were too far gone, set in their stubborn ways. Inevitably, God's judgements eventually fell, and the Kingdom of Judah was terminated (see Ezekiel 21:27).

The weeping prophet is Jeremiah's nickname. While he mourned for the people, it's likely he also wept for himself occasionally. The book of Lamentations is a testament to this assertion.

Another reason for his tears was this: in forty years of intense ministry, he is said to have had no converts, not even a single one. He had no followers to speak of, but, as the impact of his legacy attests, he definitely wasn't "just talking a walk."

Leonardo da Vinci, 1452-1519

Leonardo da Vinci, hailed as one of the most brilliant thinkers in history, was equally revered as an artist. Among his notable works are *The Mona Lisa* and *The Last Supper*. Additionally, da Vinci excelled as an architect, musician, philosopher, and scientist. His investigations spanned across geology, botany, hydraulics, mechanics, anatomy, and mathematics.

In addition to his other skills, he also possessed expertise in military engineering, city planning, mapmaking, and even aviation. By studying the flight patterns of birds and insects for years, he created an aircraft four centuries ahead of the Wright brothers. The first military tank, roller bearings, the pocket handkerchief, and the wheelbarrow were all his inventions. In his journals, he left behind 7,500 pages of innovative observations.

Nevertheless, despite his outstanding lifelong accomplishments, few are familiar with the serious social and professional hardships Leonardo encountered in his 20s and 30s. For instance, did you know that Leonardo didn't achieve major success until he completed *The Last Supper* at the tender age of 46 years old?

One of his biographers mentioned that da Vinci, who remained unmarried, experienced profound loneliness. Yet, he did not fear it. He recognized that solitary moments were catalysts for his creativity.

Indeed, we are still reaping the rewards of da Vinci's lonely years, determination, and spirit of leadership half a millennium later. Instead of worrying about his lack of followers, he cherished these times of solitude—becoming a leader in multiple fields. Making lemonade out of lemons, he redeemed the time.

Leonardo himself said, *"If you are alone, you belong entirely to yourself. If you are accompanied by even one companion you belong only half to yourself or even less in proportion to the thoughtlessness of his conduct and if you have more than one companion you will fall more deeply into the same plight."*

George Frideric Handel, 1685-1759

In an article by Christianity Today, we read: *"By 1741 George Frideric Handel was a failure. Bankrupted, in great physical pain, and the victim of plots to sabotage his career, the once-great opera composer scheduled a "farewell" appearance in London in April. To the London elite, it looked like this "German nincompoop," as he was once called, was through. That summer, however, he composed 'Messiah', which not only brought him back into the spotlight, but is still deemed by some to be 'an epitome of Christian faith.'"*

So, while Handel did have quite a following for a time, it had dwindled and almost died out by the time he wrote *Messiah*. And the rest, as they say, is history.

Walter Hunt, 1796-1859

To this day, he remains relatively unknown, despite being an innovative American mechanic and inventor. And what a prodigious inventor!

Through the course of his life's work, he became renowned for being a prolific inventor, notably of:

- The lockstitch sewing machine.
- The safety pin.
- The forerunner of the Winchester repeating rifle.
- A successful flax spinner.
- The knife sharpener.

- The streetcar bell.
- The hard-coal-burning stove.
- Artificial stone.
- Street sweeping machinery.
- The ice plow.

Regrettably, Walter Hunt failed to recognize the importance of several of his remarkable inventions. Today, many are widely used products. For sure, he didn't place enough value on the safety pin, selling the patent to W. R. Grace and Company for $400 to settle a $15 debt (which was a large amount at the time).

There are also claims that he did not patent his sewing machine out of fear that it would result in unemployment for seamstresses. This concern for others, coupled with his lack of marketing savvy and entrepreneurial spirit, led to an 1854 court case when the machine was re-invented by Elias Howe; who showed Hunt's machine to have design flaws which limited its practical use.

Walter Hunt was definitely a leader among inventors, and yet he hardly had any recognition in his day, let alone followers.

Edgar Allan Poe, 1809-1849

When thinking of Edgar Allan Poe, the celebrated American author of macabre and mystery, his troubled persona overshadows any perception of him as a leader.

Nevertheless, Poe established himself as a groundbreaking figure and visionary in literature. Although he gained fame for his horror stories, he also penned satires, humorous tales, and hoaxes. Additionally, he worked as a literary critic. The nickname "Tomahawk Man" was given to him for his brutally honest reviews.

Also, contrary to popular belief, the well-known eerie portrait of Poe (provided here) fails to capture his true likeness. He was anything but a pushover.

Poe's time in England transformed him from a frail child to a strong individual through the exercise program in schools.

Biographer Suzanne LeVert wrote, *"When he returned to Richmond with his family in 1820, he became a leader among his boyhood friends. His athletic exploits became legendary."*

In reality, he was an exceptionally athletic and attractive all-around athlete, even setting a record for swimming six miles against the tide in the James River in Virginia.

Nevertheless, Poe is included here as a leader without followers since he faced many difficulties in making a living as a writer—which was his highest gift.

The Raven, now one of the most popular poems worldwide, earned him a mere $9, but is regularly recited and used by schoolteachers. In his lifetime, Poe earned a mere $6,200 from his literary work, encompassing his fiction, poetry, criticism, and lectures. When adjusted for inflation, this amounts to approximately $191,087. Although this appears to be a substantial amount, remember that we are discussing earnings accumulated over the span of two decades.

Some of Poe's thoughts on the harshness of life are very deep, as the following line taken from his short story, *Eleonora*, indicates:

"Never to suffer would never to have been blessed."

Poe was perceived as a man wrestling with deep melancholy and treacherous inner demons. Many scholars believe he suffered from bipolar disorder. Edgar Allan Poe was nonetheless a leader in his field who, among his contemporaries, lacked the following, respect, and admiration he deserved.

Henry David Thoreau, 1817-1862

Known today as one of America's greatest philosophers ever, and one of the greatest minds and most moral men America has produced, Henry David Thoreau's books did not sell well. His contemporaries failed to fully grasp Thoreau's true nature and worth.

As a result, only two of his books got published while he was alive. According to certain scholars, the man was ahead of his time. This isn't too far off, as I believe Thoreau is still ahead, even in our time.

In his own journal (October 28, 1853), he wrote the following:

"For a year or two, my publisher, falsely so called, has been writing from time to time to ask what disposition should be made of 'A Week on the Concord and Merrimack Rivers' (Thoreau's first book) still on hand, and at last suggesting that he had use for the room they occupied in his cellar. So I had them all sent to me here, and they have arrived to-day by express, filling the man's wagon, —706 copies out of an edition of 1000 which I bought of Munroe four years ago and have ever since been paying for, and have not quite paid for yet. The wares are sent to me at last, and I have an opportunity to examine my purchase. They are something more substantial than fame, as my back knows, which has borne them up two flights of stairs to a place similar to that to which they trace their origin. Of the remaining two hundred and ninety and odd, seventy-five were given away, the rest sold. I have now a library of nearly nine hundred volumes, over seven hundred of which I wrote myself."

Ironically, his literature has been said to have inspired many other leaders, such as Mahatma Gandhi and Leo Tolstoy.

One of his most famous, inspiring, and beloved quotes is from his bestselling book, *Walden*:

"If one advances confidently in the direction of his dreams, and endeavors to live the life which he has imagined, he will meet with a success unexpected in common hours."

Thoreau was unquestionably a leader, despite not having many followers during his era.

Gregor Johann Mendel, 1822-1884

Despite his death in 1884, Mendel's significant contributions as a scientist went unrecognized until the 20th century.

Gregor Mendel gained posthumous fame as the founder of the modern science of *genetics*.

By conducting experiments with pea plants in his monastery garden, he made the groundbreaking discovery of the basic principles of heredity, which unfortunately were largely misunderstood by his contemporaries in the scientific community. Today, he has two laws named after him, both dealing with genetics.

He, too, was leading the way in his field. However, as a leader, he faced the unfortunate reality of having very few followers in his time.

Emily Dickinson, 1830-1886

The works of Emily Dickinson that described her personal thoughts on life, mortality, and nature only came to light after her death in 1886.

Emily Dickinson was an introverted hermit. She spent most of her life sheltered in her family's home in Amherst, Massachusetts. She barely published any of her poems during her lifetime. When she passed away, her sister, Lavina, uncovered 40 hand-bound volumes of her poems, totaling nearly 1,800, and arranged for their publication.

Some argue that romantic heartbreak influenced her writing style to be highly personal and centered around her own life events.

Our first impression of the woman doesn't suggest that she is a leader in any capacity. After all, out of the 1800+ poems she wrote, less than twelve were published before she died.

But, although Dickinson's life was quiet and uneventful, her writing sure wasn't. It was, in one word, *revolutionary*. Her unconventional and gloomy style was a stark contrast to the beautiful sonnets of her peers. Here's a stanza from one of her most famous poems, *I heard a Fly buzz - when I died*:

I heard a Fly buzz - when I died -
The Stillness in the Room
Was like the Stillness in the Air -
Between the Heaves of Storm -

This type of somber poetry was unheard of during that era, particularly from timid, reclusive, single women. So, unintentionally or not, Dickinson's work pushed the boundaries of society, contemporary poetry, and even grammar.

Shy and reserved? Definitely. A recognized leader in the literary world, and respected by others in the field? Definitely not in her time.

Was she nonetheless a *leader in the field of poetry*? Undoubtedly! And she is recognized as such today.

Vincent van Gogh, 1853-1890

I refer to him so much in this book because, believe it or not, despite his quirkiness, Van Gogh is the epitome of a *leader without followers*. While the Dutch painter is not known as a leader of men, he was definitely a leader in his area of gifting, i.e. painting.

Wikipedia describes him this way:

"Van Gogh was a Dutch Post-Impressionist painter who is among the most famous and influential figures in the history of Western art. In just over a decade, he created about 2,100 artworks, including around 860 oil paintings, most of them in the last two years of his life. They include landscapes, still lifes, portraits and self-

portraits, and are characterised by bold colours and dramatic, impulsive and expressive brushwork that contributed to the foundations of modern art."

What is most interesting about this man is the following:

- He had a zealous Christian faith. In a blog titled: *Vincent van Gogh's unappreciated journey with Christ*, Mark Ellis notes:

"As Vincent's zeal for Christ grew in his early twenties, he wanted to study theology, but failed his entrance exam for seminary. Instead, he went off to serve as a missionary to coal miners in the Borinage district of Belgium. He found miners who were sick and starving, living a bleak existence, without adequate food, water or warm clothing. A mining explosion had left many in a horrible condition. Fighting for survival, they apparently had little interest in his evangelistic appeals. In response to their plight, Vincent gave away everything he owned, including most of his clothing. To tend to their medical needs, he ripped up his own bed sheets for bandages, and slept on straw on the ground."

And, William J. Havlicek notes in the book *Van Gogh's Untold Journey:*

"By such actions he won the admiration and respect of the workers, and was able to convert some of them," The church board responsible for him fired him from the mission field because they thought he was (get this): *too zealous*, and because he did not dress or preach eloquently. Yes, they were, for all intents and purposes, typical Pharisees.

- He understood a lot more about leadership and gaining the trust of others than we give him credit for. He once wrote himself about how to influence people (chiefly for the Gospel, but good for all):

"One has to understand the miners' temperament and nature and approach them without pretensions, pride or a sense of superiority, otherwise one can't get on with them and can never win their trust."

Furthermore, if you wish to read some inspiring thoughts, I encourage you to read some of Vincent Van Gogh's quotes. The man was a gifted spiritual leader and philosopher.

- He died from a suspected suicide at 37 years old from a gunshot wound to the heart. There is speculation that he was possibly shot by young troublemakers in the forest. Although the nature of his death remains unclear, I believe this man, who was way ahead of his time, ultimately died of a hemorrhaging, broken, and grieving heart—overwhelmed by how hard his life was, and underwhelmed by how it had turned out.

In one of his many letters to his beloved brother, Theo, he wrote the following entry in 1882, betraying a deep melancholy:

"What am I in the eyes of most people? A nonentity or an oddity or a disagreeable person—someone who has and will have no position in society, in short, a little lower than the lowest.

Very well—assuming that everything is indeed like that, then through my work I'd like to show what there is in the heart of such an oddity, such a nobody.

Even though I'm often in a mess, inside me there's still a calm, pure harmony and music. In the poorest little house, in the filthiest corner, I see paintings or drawings. And my mind turns in that direction as if with an irresistible urge."

Sadly, Van Gogh died broken… and broke. He sold only one painting during his lifetime: *Red Vineyard at Arles.*

Of his art not selling, he said, *"I can't change the fact that my paintings don't sell. But the time will come when people will recognize that they are worth more than the value of the paints used in the picture."*

His words proved prophetic. The rest of Van Gogh's more than 900 paintings were not sold or made famous until *after his death* by his sister-in-law. Furthermore, he generated a multitude of drawings and sketches, amounting to almost one new piece of art every 36 hours. Alongside his vast collection of artworks, Van Gogh also wrote an almost equal number of letters and postcards.

So, who knows, maybe this leader without followers never followed his true destiny. We can only hypothesize that perhaps he felt betrayed by the Church and under-used by God to a point where he just couldn't stand it anymore. It is, for sure, a most tragic story.

Nikola Tesla, 1856-1943

One of the more tragic stories ever in the realm of innovation, invention, and leadership of one's gift, is the case of Nikola Tesla.

While he is recognized today for his unparalleled genius along with everything he contributed to mankind, Tesla's life was marked by a constant struggle against adversity. Sadly, he would never fully overcome his many setbacks.

A great light was given to mankind when he was born, but many servants of darkness did everything they could to keep it from shining. Indeed, the elite have no incentive to support free energy if it threatens their control over the 99%. So, over and over during his lifetime, Tesla was taken advantage of by ruthless businessmen.

Furthering his own demise, Tesla had the tendency to be more concerned with blueprints than with contracts. While he was a genius, paperwork pertaining to business was not his forte.

After a life spent in the relentless pursuit of innovation, and after having been swindled by many shrewd and wealthy elites, he died penniless, insane, and alone in a New York city hotel room. At one of his lowest points, Nikola Tesla, arguably the smartest man on earth at the time, dug ditches for $2 a day to make ends meet.

But, to his credit, he possessed an affable, persistent, and forgiving nature. The greatest saying of this leader without followers is undoubtedly:

"I don't care that they stole my idea, I care that they don't have any of their own." ~Nikola Tesla

I could also list many other leaders without followers who, although they impacted people and history, only did so posthumously: Oscar Wilde (bankrupt at the time of his death), John Keats (whose poems were unappreciated except among close friends), or even Mozart (who died uncelebrated, without friends or close ones, and was buried in an unmarked grave).

My friend, Roger Hataway, 1938-2012

One of the greatest theological minds I have ever encountered is a man unknown to most, and uncelebrated. Roger Hataway never graduated from seminary. He doesn't have a book to his name. He never taught in any school. You won't find him on YouTube or elsewhere expounding his fascinating theories and findings.

Roger Hataway was a very humble and quiet man whose joy stemmed from a simple life with his beloved wife, piety, and research. He made his home in rural Virginia.

Despite his unassuming life, I would never dare to question this man's leadership and wisdom. He had a tremendous impact on me by showing me a living example of what a committed life to Christ looks like. His blend of knowledge, leadership, and humility amazed me.

To this day, his greatest legacy is a website that his family maintains at: http://www.divinepageant.com/.

This is where he documented all of his research and writing—offering it freely to the world. Keep in mind that browsing the website might expose you to content that could be considered controversial or even offensive. So, consider yourself forewarned.

With that said, mining for truth is like mining for gold or precious stones: we must be willing to get our hands dirty to uncover those nuggets. So too, to get to the truth, we must do so through previously unexplored paths of knowledge. I always tell my audience to *"chew the grass, spit out the hay."*

I once wrote to Roger, asking him why he never got all of his research published in a book. He replied, *"Years ago I considered having "Christ's New Covenant" published in book form. Elitist book publishing companies and their gatekeepers wouldn't consider it, and I could not afford to self-publish (note that this was a decade before Amazon KDP), so I dropped the idea. Since I began publishing on the internet, I can simply run off an article on the printer when necessary. Sorry, but I don't have any stock of writing printed out, at all. And I don't have the capability of printing the entire website as one production. That would be hundreds of pages!"*

Well, regardless, I am happy to use these few lines to honor this beloved man, his leadership, and his lovingkindness.

To most, Roger was just an old man, living quietly away in the countryside, away from the hustle and bustle. But to me and a few select others, he was unique in his knowledge, understanding, wisdom, and interpretation of Scripture. Although our relationship by mail was brief, he was a mentor and an example. I have such fond memories of him! The least that can be said is that this beloved leader had at least one follower.

My friend, Roger Hataway

The Case for Christ

Here is a complex and tricky question to consider: Could Jesus Christ be considered the greatest leader without followers in history?

Now, obviously, the knee-jerk reactive answer of most in this case would be: *"There are millions of believers around the world. I think Jesus is far from being a leader without followers. Quite the contrary."*

For sure, this is a fair assessment of the Lord Jesus Christ's results as far as followers are concerned. Or is it?

Let's probe the question further, shall we?

When we consider a leader's following, we must first consider *who he is*. For instance, someone who is appointed to a high position should, in order to be considered successful at it, have a significant number of followers. For example, if a U.S. president has only a 12% approval rating (which more or less reflects his followership), is he a leader, or a leader without followers?

Let me thus play devil's advocate (a term I despise, by the way).

With Christ being the sinless Son of the Living God, and the sole appointed Savior of Mankind, providing forgiveness of sins and eternal life, shouldn't *everyone* become His follower?

This, of course, is a rhetorical question. The answer is an obvious *Yes!*

And yet, many aren't following Him. In fact, millions upon millions, for various reasons, do not follow *the ultimate leader in history*—even if they were acquainted with His words, His works, and the Gospel. The number of people who follow Christ is significantly smaller compared to those who don't, taking all the numbers into account.

Now, we know for a fact that Christ's persona and leadership are flawless. He was, after all, sinless. In an ideal world, everyone would recognize His worth and follow Him. Period.

However, even a perfect leader such as Him can face a limited number of followers. This single fact proves the imperfection of our world.

Of course, this was no surprise to Christ, who knew this would happen. Unlike many people nowadays, He didn't feel embarrassed by having a small number of followers. He didn't associate His self-worth with having a large crowd of people following Him or approving of Him.

In fact, He said, *"Remember the word that I said to you, 'A slave is not greater than his master.' If they persecuted Me, they will persecute you as well; if they followed My word, they will follow yours also."* ~John 15:20, NASB

Of all leaders lacking followers, Christ undoubtedly stood out as the greatest. The intriguing paradox of Jesus Christ is that he is simultaneously the greatest leader in history and the greatest leader lacking followers.

The One whom everyone should have followed, was actually the One most rejected. It shouldn't come as a shock, considering that the prophet Isaiah predicted it 700 years before His birth. Here's what he wrote about the Lord:

"He was despised and rejected by men, a man of sorrows and acquainted with grief; and as one from whom men hide their faces he was despised, and we esteemed him not." ~Isaiah 53:3, ESV

The following is a popular poem about the life of Jesus Christ. It is attributed to James Allen Francis, and it aptly portrays the lonely leadership journey of the ultimate leader.

One Solitary Life

"He was born in an obscure village, the child of a peasant. He grew up in another village, where he worked in a carpenter shop until he was 30. Then, for three years, he was an itinerant preacher.

He never wrote a book. He never held an office. He never had a family or owned a home. He didn't go to college. He never lived in a big city. He never traveled 200 miles from the place where he was born. He did none of the things that usually accompany greatness. He had no credentials but himself.

He was only 33 when the tide of public opinion turned against him. His friends ran away. One of them denied him. He was turned over to his enemies and went through the mockery of a trial. He was nailed to a cross between two thieves. While he was dying, his executioners gambled for his garments, the only property he had on earth. When he was dead, he was laid in a borrowed grave, through the pity of a friend.

Twenty centuries have come and gone, and today he is the central figure of the human race. I am well within the mark when I say that all the armies that ever marched, all the navies that ever sailed, all the parliaments that ever sat, all the kings that ever reigned--put together--have not affected the life of man on this earth as much as that one, solitary life."

The case for Christ as a leader without followers is, without a doubt, an interesting study. It serves, more than any other example, as an undeniable proof that followers are not a prerequisite for leadership, and that the number of people following you is not an accurate measure of the quality of your leadership in this world.

The Characteristics of LWF's

The men and women addressed in this chapter became leaders without followers for the following reasons:

- **Most of them were *thought-leaders.*** They say ideas (thoughts) make the world go 'round. Great ideas are what leads innovation and forward progress.

- **They were *leaders in their area of gifting*** who marched forward and did their thing, regardless of followers.

- **Many were *leaders ahead of their time*,** and thus mostly unappreciated during their time.

- **They were *ground-breaking trailblazers*,** and people were unfamiliar and cautious of the new territory these ground-breaking trailblazers were exploring.

- **God chose some for a specific purpose;** all they needed to do was answer the call, use their gift, and not worry about the consequences or their number of followers.

- **Their gifts were their legacy.** Those who became famous posthumously were leaders whose gifts were only appreciated later.

Regardless of one's opinion about him, Nietzsche made a valid point with his statement: *"My time has not yet come either; some are born posthumously."*

So, dear reader, it's possible that you, too, were born posthumously. Is it conceivable that your lack of followers isn't indicative of a failure in your leadership after all? Is it possible that, perhaps, it is part of your calling to endure this lone trek? Is it possible that you are being used right now to be a trailblazer for future generations?

Often, the leaders without followers are those paving the way where there is no way yet. Unseen and uncelebrated, they are forging a path that may only be appreciated by future generations.

If that's true for you, always remember that true leadership involves planting trees without expecting to benefit from their shade. The measure of your true legacy lies in the lives touched and progress made, through the humble act of planting seeds and fostering growth.

And if you find your present lack of results discouraging and feel like giving up, consider this: The last thing to grow on a fruit tree is... the fruit.

CHAPTER 6

Leadership vs. Influence

"Without a doubt, the most common weakness of all human beings is the habit of leaving their minds open to the negative influence of other people."

~Napoleon Hill

While sharing a live teaching for the *Maximum Impact Mentoring* group in August 2020, John C. Maxwell, considered by many as the foremost expert on leadership, reflected on a statement he had previously made in his acclaimed book, *The 21 Irrefutable Laws of Leadership*.

In this book, *The Law of Influence* is recognized as the second irrefutable law of leadership.

Prior to this teaching, which was coined, *The Difference Between Leadership and Influence*, John Maxwell frequently stated that, *"Leadership is influence, nothing more, nothing less."*

But, demonstrating exceptional humility and sincerity, he declared during this live broadcast that his investigation into social media trends over the past few years invalidated this assertion.

On the teaching call, he said: *"There is a difference between influence and leadership. In fact, for me to say that, if you've read "The 21 Irrefutable Laws of Leadership", you know that one of the laws is that leadership is influence, nothing more, nothing less. And, I am saying to you that, wow… in 42 years of me leading, I look at that statement, and I ask myself, 'Is this still true? Is this truly a leadership law?'"*

As he proceeded, he added, *"Now, when I wrote that leadership is influence, nothing more, nothing less, I did it in the context of the culture at the time (the late 80's), and the intricacies of that teaching were before the context of social media. Social media has changed how many people we can influence. It has changed why we influence people. It has changed how we use our influence on people. All of that has changed because of social media.*

[…] I think much of social media is about influencing people, but I'm not so sure it's about leadership. When I lead people, it's all about people, but when I influence people on social media, it's all about me. And when leading people, good values are required. But when I'm influencing people on social media, no good values are required."

I couldn't agree more with these statements and observations.

Furthermore, I believe that influencers have unknowingly given a great deal of credibility to my theory. The truth is becoming evident for many casual observers: followers don't create or confirm leaders. They merely affirm leadership *potential*. With that said, however, when we scrutinize most social media influencers these days, we often discover that even their apparent leadership potential is merely a superficial front.

When analyzing social media 'influencers' on platforms like Instagram and TikTok, it is clear that their contributions lack long-term significance. Through their actions and superficial contributions, they present evidence that influence and leadership are not synonymous.

As someone trained by *The John Maxwell Team* in leadership and public speaking, I was thrilled to hear the founder express this ideological change. But truth be told, I had known it for some time. While I hadn't yet written about it, I had concluded that asserting *'leadership is influence, nothing more, nothing less'* was a fallacy. In fact, as a long-time leader without followers, I had experienced its falsehood firsthand. I knew it just wasn't true—even if it may have been decades prior, in one form or another, in organizational, corporate, or church settings, mostly.

Notwithstanding, there is no denying that influence still plays a huge part in defining and measuring leadership effectiveness toward people. At first glance, we can see why that is. Without a doubt, the most notable leaders in history exerted a substantial influence on individuals. In most cases, the more influence they had, the better leaders they were deemed to be, and the more followers they had.

The drawback of that concept, however, is that a person's leadership potential may rely entirely on their capacity to sway others.

By saying this, I acknowledge the need to provide further explanation.

I believe that leadership is sometimes more than mere influence, and sometimes less than influence as well. But before I go on, let's look at the definition of *influence* according to Webster's 1828 dictionary:

IN'FLUENCE, *noun* [Latin *influens, influo,* to flow in; *in* and *fluo,* to flow.] Literally, a flowing in, into or on, and referring to substances spiritual or too subtle to be visible, like inspiration. Hence, the word was formerly followed by *into.*

So, influence means *to flow into.* Someone who has influence *flows into* the minds and hearts of others and imparts desires, tastes, and actions that are usually similar to his own.

Thus, by this definition, we may affirm that influence can be positive or negative. People can exert influence over others, whether it be for good, evil, or even for neutral or insignificant thoughts, tastes, beliefs, or actions. Leadership, however, contrary to influence, must weigh heavier on the positive side of the scale.

Let me explain.

The concept of negative leadership, in a way, is an oxymoron—even though it does exist. That's why we came up with terms like *bully, dictator, despot, oppressor, tyrant, bad leader, incompetent boss,* etc. While these types of 'leaders' all exert some level of influence, would we call them leaders in the day-to-day? Not likely. I know I wouldn't.

As a rule of thumb, we instinctively associate leadership with *good leadership.* Conversely, however, influence has the potential to be either beneficial or detrimental. For instance, when we admonish our children to steer clear of a particular friend, we often say, *"He's a negative influence on you."* We wouldn't say, *"He's not the best fit as a leader for you."*

How Do You Like Them Burgers?

There's a burger restaurant that began operating in my area a few years back. Out of curiosity, I decided to visit their website when they launched, and the pictures of their gourmet burgers made my mouth water—BIG time!

Their burgers appeared massive, topped with grade 'A' ingredients, and looked extremely appetizing! Enthused, I took the initiative to share the news of the new place with my work colleagues. I shared the website and the pictures with them and guess what? It made them drool, too!

It so happened that my wife, 3-year-old daughter, and I were the first ones to have lunch at that restaurant one fateful day. As expected, their burgers were just as good as advertised. I even took pictures of my meal so that I could boast to my co-workers I had eaten there first.

When I arrived at work the following day, I shared my photos and boasted about the burgers' incredible size, appearance, and mouthwatering taste, along with the exceptional quality of the new place.

Can you guess what happened next?

In the weeks that followed, they all went, one after another, to grab a bite there. Clearly, *I influenced them* to go to that restaurant. But this begs the question: *Did I lead them?* Clearly not. While I played a significant role in motivating them to give it a shot, I wasn't explicitly leading them to do it. I didn't accompany them when they went, and I didn't hand them the specific address either.

John Maxwell once said, and it's true, that *"A leader is one who knows the way, goes the way, and shows the way."*

Well, I knew the way, but I had gone by myself, and the only thing I showed them were pictures. So, I hardly qualified as a leader in this instance.

Did I influence them? Absolutely!

Did I lead them? No.

This, clearly, was a situation where my influence didn't translate into effective leadership. And such instances are a dime a dozen, not just for me, but for everybody.

The Markers of Leadership vs. Influence

In an article titled *The One Thing You Can't Be an Effective Leader Without,* Dr. Stephen Graves identified the following insightful differences between the two:

- Leadership is visible; influence is out of sight.

- Leadership is usually conscious; influence is often unconscious.
- Leadership is contained; influence crosses boundaries.
- Leadership is immediate; influence is long term.
- Leadership is public; influence is often behind the scenes.
- Leadership is formulaic; influence is mysterious.
- Leadership captivates culture; influence drives culture.
- Leadership is the tip of the iceberg; influence is the mass under the surface.
- Leaders act on people; influence affects people and outcomes.

In the article, he also brought up this interesting point:

"Sure, you have the Abraham Lincolns of the world who are influential leaders. But for every Abraham Lincoln, you have a Vincent van Gogh, Franz Schubert, and Karl Marx—people of massive influence who had no leadership position and even died in obscurity."

Okay, just for the record, I am glad Marx died in obscurity—and he should have stayed there. But I digress.

As I mentioned earlier, I strongly believe that the aforementioned people were, despite their lack of followers, *leaders in their area of gifting.*

I also believe Shakespeare knew something of the difference between leaders and influencers when he wrote in *Twelfth Night*: *"Some are born great, some achieve greatness, and some have greatness thrust upon them."*

The ultimate achievement for a leader is, of course, to possess both strong leadership *and* influence ability. Fulfilled potential is usually achieved when an individual possesses both *the spirit of leadership* and a great deal of influence.

You see, influence is the unique quality of leadership that actually fosters a following. It could be argued then, that leaders can possess varying levels of influence.

Nevertheless, with that said, not all good leaders have influence and many influencers do not lead people. They are more similar to effective salespeople.

All of Life is Sales

Is the development of influence important for leaders? No doubt about it! Think of the impact it would have made in the life of Van Gogh, Emily Dickinson, Nikola Tesla, or perhaps even Noah to develop a higher capacity to influence others.

The late Jim Rohn, who was known as a motivational speaker and business philosopher, once expressed the notion that *all of life is sales*. Observing the lack of response from the audience, combined with their potential skepticism, he then explained further, stating:

- We sell our competence when going for a job interview.

- We sell our worth when trying to woo someone of the opposite sex.
- We sell our products or services when we have a business.
- We sell our point of view every day when trying to get our point across during a conversation.
- We sell our preference when trying to convince friends to go to a certain restaurant or movie.

Additionally, I would include in that list the fact that we also engage in sales, to some degree at least, when presenting the gospel to various individuals. Indeed, in our daily lives, we constantly perform as salesmen. We sell our ideas, plans, and enthusiasm to everyone we meet. All of life, therefore, is sales. And how would you define sales in the simplest way? It is *influence*.

While your ability to influence others may or may not be connected to your personal leadership mojo, you'll quickly see how it can impact your sales success.

For leaders, especially introverted ones like myself, the challenge lies in mastering the ability to influence (or sell). Failing to do so often leads to a shortage of followers, customers, or income.

So, yes, the truth is that sales is life, and life is sales. If you see a separation, chances are you are already one step behind.

The Lord Jesus proposed a simple principle that supports this seemingly awkward notion when He said:

"Ask and it will be given to you; seek and you will find; knock and the door will be opened to you. 8 For everyone who asks receives; the one who seeks finds; and to the one who knocks, the door will be opened." ~Matthew 7:7-8, NIV

Now, you might say, *"But often I've asked, sought, and knocked with no apparent results or even outright refusals. How do you explain that?"*

Well, what would have happened if you hadn't asked or knocked? Nothing. Guaranteed. So, this Scripture is also saying conversely: Don't ask, don't get. Or, in the words of Wayne Gretzky's father, Walter, *"You miss 100% of the shots you don't take."*

Entrepreneur, author, and motivational speaker Jack Canfield summed it up well when he said:

"If you are not moving closer to what you want in sales (or in life), you probably aren't doing enough asking."

Now, let's move on to the next logical question: *when should we ask?* Simple. Only once you've helped someone is it okay to ask.

I love how Mary Kay Ash, founder of Mary Kay cosmetics, put it. She said:

"Pretend that every single person you meet has a sign around his or her neck that says, 'Make me feel important.' Not only will you succeed in sales, but you will also succeed in life."

That, dear friend, is the recipe for influence and sales. It is that simple. It is that hard.

Are You a Leader, an Influencer, or a Leader with Influence?

This brings us to a nuanced understanding of the distinct categories that exist among leaders, leaders of people, and influencers. But I think it's time for a bit of a refresher.

As we've explored, a *leader* is not exclusively someone with followers; it is an individual who navigates their own life with clarity, recognizing their gifts and purpose. Such leaders develop and serve their gifts with a sense of purpose, striving to make a difference, whether or not they accumulate a substantial following. These are the individuals to whom I've dedicated this book—those who embody *the spirit of leadership*, often without the fanfare of followers or significant influence.

A *leader of people*, on the other hand, is characterized by the ability to guide and lead others in various settings, such as business, organizations, churches, or social environments. Whether possessing an innate talent for leadership or whether bestowed with a distinct spiritual gift, these individuals stand out for their capacity to effectively guide, influence, and lead people through diverse projects, seasons, or transitions. They represent the traditional leaders we've been taught to emulate, offering a comprehensive package of leadership qualities and achieving tangible results.

In this chapter, we've considered how a novel archetype has emerged in our day and age: the *influencer*.

These individuals, in the modern sense, occupy a unique space: social media. The prevailing definition identifies influencers as individuals who wield the power to impact others' decisions due to their authority, knowledge, position, affluence, and/or relationship with their audience. Influencers engage actively with their niche following.

The combination of leadership and influence can be described as embodying the best of both worlds, becoming an *influential leader*. We should all strive for this, as it brings forth the best in ourselves and, on the whole, may affect individuals positively in a world that desperately needs good role models.

The upcoming chapter will delve into the diverse nature of online influencers, revealing how some leverage their influence for positive causes, while others steer followers in less favorable directions.

It is worth noting again that a brief online search for the current top influencers raises concerns about the impact these figures might have on our youth, our society, and our future. The disconcerting results found when googling 'top influencers today' offer a stark reminder that our societal landscape is, for the most part, not characterized by much rationality.

Innovation: The Path of Most Resistance

The best leaders are trailbreakers, innovators, often making a way where there is no way, breaking new grounds and showing others that it can, in fact, be done. The negative perception of this 'can do' attitude by others contributes to the difficulty of gaining followers. The majority of individuals avoid getting their hands dirty. So, staying back, they prefer to casually observe those who bravely venture out and attempt to make a way where it seems impossible.

Like him or not, the co-founder of Apple computers, Steve Jobs, was spot on when he said, *"Innovation distinguishes between a leader and a follower."*

The role of innovation is a critical factor that sets leaders apart from followers, and even from influencers. Leadership, at its core, involves actively engaging in the pursuit of new ideas, solutions, and approaches to challenges, and perhaps even, to a lesser extent, to the norms. Many influencers don't fit that bill. They often prefer to market things already at their disposal to create their impact. They conveniently choose the path of less resistance, often opting to market, recycle, or repackage rather than innovate. They rarely, if ever, break new grounds.

Leaders, however, are characterized by their forward-thinking mindset and their ability to embrace and drive innovation. They are not content with the status quo; instead, they actively seek for ways and opportunities to break away from conventional thinking. Innovation thus becomes a defining trait of those with *the spirit of leadership* as they navigate uncertainties, solve complex problems, create new products, and steer themselves and their ideas or organizations toward growth and success.

This distinction of leaders lies in a deep hunger, often unexplainable, that transpires as a willingness to take risks, often big ones, and explore uncharted territories. Driven by a hunger for innovation, leaders are unafraid to challenge the status quo and push boundaries of what is familiar, proven, and/or even esteemed.

Challenging the status quo by pushing limitations frequently brings leaders to question established norms, prompting those in authority to harbor a contempt and even hatred—especially when these innovations have more to do with changing mindsets and societal norms.

Historical examples vividly illustrate the dire consequences faced by those who pushed against entrenched beliefs, with figures like the Lord Jesus Christ, His apostles, Martin Luther King, and even JFK (who, as some believe, wanted to abolish the Federal Reserve, which led to his demise), immediately coming to mind, among many others. All of them desired to bring significant change and took steps to do so. And all of them paid a steep price for it.

The Myth of the 24-Hour Leader

In our day and age, with content regularly going viral on social media, many can end up as overnight celebrity influencers, garnering much attention and a massive following in the process. In today's flawed understanding of leadership, the perception is, essentially, that having a substantial number of followers overnight immediately transforms one into a leader.

But does it? This notion begs some further investigation.

If someone on social media goes from 100 followers to 10,000 followers *overnight,* does that make them a leader? And if so, what changed? Has the quality of their leadership improved? What of their level of integrity? Are they now considered leaders because their followership grew?

Obviously, the truth is that *nothing has changed*. Their social media handles haven't changed. Their persona, leadership and integrity haven't changed in 24 hours. And yet, despite no change whatsoever to *who they are*, the *perception* of who they are has now been dramatically transformed. So, how do we explain this modern phenomenon?

Popular personal growth author, life coach, and podcaster Mastin Kipp's journey and testimony serves as an interesting example of this strange reality.

Years ago, after overcoming addiction and losing his dream job in the music industry, Mastin Kipp launched TheDailyLove.com (at the time) to connect with like-minded individuals. Aside from a challenging start that took him a year to gain a thousand followers on social media, Kipp also faced personal setbacks, including a failed relationship, financial difficulties, and even health issues.

Undeterred, he continued working on his blog and Twitter account, even moving into a tiny pool house to make ends meet. Now practically homeless, his dedication paid off when a tweet from Kim Kardashian (not an endorsement), who then had over a million followers on social media, catapulted TheDailyLove.com from one thousand to 10,000 followers—literally overnight.

Did Mastin Kipp undergo a sudden transformation that made him more deserving of a bigger following? Obviously, the answer is no. Even he would agree. He was still the same guy as the day before, down on his luck and living in that pool house, but he had just won the follower lottery through something unexpected. I had the pleasure of listening to Mastin Kipp's unique testimony. As far as I can gather, he seems like a genuinely smart and kind man, so good on him. But the point, once again, is that in the age of influence your followership, or lack thereof, is no indicator of your quality as a leader.

The testimony of Mastin Kipps testifies to three things:

1. You can be unknown, hidden from view, and yet highly valuable.
2. Your number of followers has nothing to do with your true worth.
3. The *spirit of leadership* you carry is often the result of years of painful hardship and toil.

Another phenomenon is also observable in this case: i.e. highly competent and deserving leaders can be left to rot for an indeterminate period through no fault of their own.

One of the most intelligent and capable leaders in history was, without a doubt, Joseph, in the Old Testament. Wherever he found himself, the spirit of leadership he carried was such that he quickly rose to prominence—whether it was as a slave in Potiphar's household (Genesis 39:4-6), or as a prisoner in jail (39:21-23). His overseers simply recognized his superior managerial ability, integrity, and intellect. And, let's not forget, the story tells us the Lord was also with him (Genesis 39:21).

Nevertheless, as we have seen, Joseph was either a slave or prisoner for thirteen years of his life. This, of course, is not a reflection of his true capacity as a leader.

Just like Mastin Kipp, Joseph became an *overnight success* when he was given an audience with the king of Egypt (the Pharaoh) to interpret his dream. He rose to prominence after being endorsed by a prominent man. And the rest, as they say, is history.

The point to all of this is that no matter who social media promotes and makes viral, there is no such thing as a 24-hour leader. Mastin Kipp already carried within himself the ingredients, insights, and depth that enabled him to get to a higher position in life, and to an even greater extent, so did Joseph.

The world may acknowledge your years of development in a mere second. Once it does, everything takes a turn. Proper handling of this success, however, is reserved for those who have paid their dues.

As some successful people like to say, *"It took me years to become an overnight success."* And yet, in the age of social media and influence, it can take some mere seconds. Nevertheless, it is likely that those influencers who achieved success in seconds will fade into obscurity just as quickly.

As the saying goes, *"Talent will get you in the door, but character will keep you in the room."* And you can't microwave character.

Chance Favors the Bold… and the Beautiful

Here is another question to ponder: Does social media offer a fair chance to anybody and everybody to exert influence? The answer is a convoluted, *yes* and *no*.

The opportunity is there for everyone, obviously. However, as some commercials often state, *results may vary.*

Similar to TV professionals, social media influencers benefit from having charisma, presence, and an attractive appearance. The media has shaped our expectations by consistently featuring attractive individuals in movies, TV, and magazines.

It's no wonder, then, that numerous influential and successful social media personalities are attractive, especially the ladies. So, the question of fairness is irrelevant when faced with reality. In cases of equal talent, content, or product quality, people are more likely to gravitate towards attractive people rather than unattractive ones. Humans, after all, are visual creatures.

Even the Bible reminds us of this. When the prophet Samuel was sent to Jesse's (David's father) household to anoint the next king of Israel, he was first swayed by the physical appearance of David's elder brother, thinking he was surely the one to be anointed as king. But the Lord reminded Samuel," Do *not look at his appearance or at his physical stature, because I have refused him. For the Lord does not see as man sees; for man looks at the outward appearance, but the Lord looks at the heart."* ~1 Samuel 16:7, NKJV

Regardless, there is undoubtedly a relationship between good looks and one's impact on social media.

What I am saying is this: some people get more opportunities, exert wider influence, and attract more followers simply because they are, well, *more attractive.*

It seems unfair, doesn't it? That's because it is.

In a society that claims to value inclusiveness and equality, this might offend some people. Believe me, I am not trying to be offensive here; just realistic. The point is: attractiveness is, well, *attractive*. Good looks make you look good. And, sure enough, sex appeal... *appeals*.

An article in the magazine *Business Insider* presented the results of scientific studies on the effects of beauty. Here is a rundown of what they found:

1. Beautiful people are viewed as healthier.
2. Beautiful people are actually healthier.
3. It's easier for beautiful people to find mates.
4. Beautiful people are (perceived as) more intelligent.
5. Beautiful people are more persuasive.
6. Companies with good-looking executives have higher sales.
7. Beautiful people have an advantage in politics.
8. Beautiful people are perceived as more likeable and trustworthy.

You can check out the full article here: http://www.businessinsider.com/studies-show-the-advantages-of-being-beautiful-2013-6

The conclusion is this: Good-looking people are more attractive, influential, and therefore *attract more followers*. Period.

Before anyone boldly enters the fray of social media marketing, they need to be aware of this fact. And yes, it is a *fact*—albeit an unfortunate one.

Nevertheless, I do not wish here to be misunderstood. So, let me clarify further.

If you weren't highly favored by the genetic lottery, and you have, as one of my entrepreneur friends once said, *a face tailor-made for radio*, you can't let that stop you. You can still attract legions of followers, even raving fans, through the quality of your knowledge, teachings, products, services, likeability, or your ability to connect with people. Heck, you can even attract followers *because* you are different! Just consider popular speaker and author Nick Vujicic, who, because he is different (having been born with no arms and no legs), has built a significant platform from which he influences others, preaching the gospel and teaching young people all over the world.

In like manner, you must leverage your strengths and uniqueness. And that requires much work. So, attractiveness isn't the end-all be-all definer of your followership or mine. It just tends to help, that's all.

Conversely, if you are blessed with physical attractiveness, do not let this be your downfall.

What do I mean? Well, while people may at first follow you for your buy-in factor, you can be sure they'll cease following you if they see you do not deliver the goods. Whether you look like a superstar or not, you still have to deliver rockstar products, services, or content. At the end of the day, lasting success, leadership, and influence are all about adding value—genuine value.

Faded Stars

To underscore the concept that influence doesn't automatically equate to leadership, consider once more the pervasive impact of pop culture and social media 'stars,' whom I'll refrain from naming to sidestep potential legal issues.

These cultural figures wield global influence through various channels, such as clothing, fashion products, media appearances, music, and art. However, when examined through the lens of intrinsic leadership values, they fall short of meeting the criteria. Their influence aligns more with Jack London's notion that *"Affluence is influence."* And while some may disagree with this cynical perspective, I am comfortable standing by it.

It is crucial to recognize the difference between conventional leadership and the attraction of popularity or influence, especially in relation to the prominence of Hollywood, pop culture, fashion, and the prevalence of social media.

Two hundred years ago, it might have been challenging to differentiate between influence and leadership. Back then, media stars were virtually nonexistent, and influencers belonged to a distinct category, which included politicians, clergy, teachers, intellectuals, and authors—individuals more readily identified as leaders in the traditional sense.

Thus, I believe the demarcation between leadership and influence has become more pronounced with the elevation of Hollywood, consumerism, and social media's prominence in our culture. Since then, we've witnessed the emergence of *numerous influencers*, much at the expense of traditional leaders as we once recognized them.

Reflecting on this fact, it becomes apparent that the distinction between leadership and influence has, as John Maxwel observed, evolved—even morphed. While leadership and influence are intertwined and occasionally used interchangeably, they are now distinct concepts. Recognizing this difference is paramount if one aspires to be both a leader and an influencer.

Become Independently Influent

As I close this chapter on the differences between influence and leadership, I feel one truth become clear above all else. There exists a tension for leaders, a dichotomy of sorts, a median line that we must skillfully navigate—like a funambulist walking a tightrope.

On the one hand, your leadership growth journey requires you to positively influence others, be it through sales, innovation, service, or teaching. Developing a healthy level of influence is both necessary and beneficial for achieving this. That's why we strive to better ourselves at extending our influence though networking, whether in person or online, advertising, making videos, writing books, developing our public speaking, etc.

We do these things because we firmly believe in the power of our knowledge, products, and/or skill to make a real difference in people's lives. In this way, we push ourselves to become more influential, which in turn helps us create a more significant impact.

On the other hand, however, we understand that the end goal isn't influence for its own sake, or amassing a certain number of followers. We seek to make a difference, hopefully influencing and transforming lives, but we cannot determine how many lives will be affected, nor should we make numbers our goal. There must, therefore, with the spirit of leadership, come an acceptance that ultimately, our life, our work, and its impact are in God's hands. There is a detachment that comes from this acceptance. A freeing sentiment, even.

Therefore, at the end of the day...

- We aim to become more influent, but we do not make influence our aim.
- We strive to reach more people, but we do not get offended if we don't.
- We offer to add value to people, but we do not feel devalued if they refuse.
- We invest in ways to bring our message, service, or product available to more people, but we do not do it merely to attract more followers.
- We aim to please, but we avoid becoming people-pleasers.

- We hope to have a positive impact on individuals and possibly influence them, but we remain independent and dedicated to our calling and the Caller.

By doing so, may you achieve both independence and influence, while staying true to yourself, your calling, and your Father in heaven.

In the upcoming chapter, we'll delve deeper into effectively navigating social media and expanding your influence by weighing both its inherent risks and rewards.

CHAPTER 7

Social Media and Influence

"Social media is about sociology and psychology more than technology."

~Brian Solis

In a 2023 interview titled *'How to Destroy Your Negative Beliefs'*, found on YouTube, renowned Canadian psychologist and social commentator Jordan Peterson, was asked by the host:

"You say, 'You are morally obligated to do remarkable things.' Why?"

Peterson paused, his eyes shifting downward, deep in thought. He then raised his gaze and gave an absolutely epic reply (partially printed here):

"Well, I think, partly, because life is so difficult and challenging, that unless you give it everything you have, the chances

are very high that it will embitter you. And then you'll be a force for darkness, and not good. […]

So, why is that a moral obligation? Well, if you hide and you don't let what's inside of you out—and you don't bring into the world what you could bring—you become cynical and bitter. Not only will you not add to the world what you could add, but you'll start being jealous of people who are competent and doing well and work to destroy them. That's the pathway to hell."

Dear leader, I concur with Dr. Peterson, a man I respect for his forthrightness and profound insights. Indeed, *it is your moral obligation to do remarkable things*. It is your duty to let your light and the truth shine out. You must do that remarkable thing, and then do everything in your power to share it with the world. Period.

The failure of some leaders to attract any followers, as highlighted in previous chapters, is often attributed to their inability and/or commitment to share their gift adequately. Therefore, many individuals today still, are unable to gain attention, followers, and find success. As Peterson observed, some of these leaders chose to remain in isolation and avoidance, i.e. Van Gogh and Emily Dickinson, to name just two. Notwithstanding, their gifts were so potent (even necessary), that the world eventually took notice and shared their fruit, albeit, sadly, posthumously.

As leaders, we thus find ourselves trapped in a delicate equilibrium. *On the one hand,* we have a moral obligation from our Creator to develop and generously share our gift with the world.

On the other hand, we don't want to do it solely to gather followers and/or to become famous. Rather, we aim to share our light with humanity and, hopefully, make a meaningful impact. It is our dutiful purpose. We wish to do so because, *yes;* it is part of our moral obligation, and yet we also wish to remain humble throughout this self-promotion process.

And so, dear leader, we find that the best way to share our gift nowadays is through *social media.*

Therein lies the challenge.

Social media is made in such a way that the goal of the game seems to be to gather as many followers as possible. It seems like there has never been a more perfect platform for satisfying one's ego bestowed upon humanity. Many who engage in it lie and cheat to get ahead. And the worse part is that they do! So, while social media provides an amazing opportunity for anyone to grow their influence and share product, thoughts, and/or service with the world, it is also a festering swamp that breeds narcissism on a global scale.

Dear leader, welcome to the age of influence and the world of social media PR and marketing.

Follow Me On...

The term *follower* has become a household name for social media lingo. In fact, the tendency to value people's worth and leadership by how many followers they have on X, or Facebook, or Instagram, or TikTok has only worsened with the skyrocketing popularity of social media.

I must confess, I'm actually at fault for this as well. I tend to trust individuals, products, and companies with larger followings, likes, or positive reviews. In all fairness, the reason we do this is to safeguard ourselves and efficiently find top-notch products or services. It's natural to do so, and safer, but not always accurate. It's not always advantageous, whether we consider it from an individual or societal perspective.

As I said before, people are a bunch of *flockers*. And there's no place they flock to more than social media.

We are like sheep and we stick together. The bigger the crowd, we reason, the lesser the chance of being deceived, or defrauded. Like I said, I do it too. Whenever I look for a video on YouTube, I often click on the one with the most views. I often joke with the kids, *"Can't go wrong with one million views"* (or two, or three). But, every so often, when doing research, I purposely select videos or blogs with low view counts. In doing so, I have often been blessed with surprisingly innovative content or ideas, which I would not have found otherwise.

I like Mark Twain's reflection on the potential folly of following the crowd. He said:

"Whenever you find yourself on the side of the majority, it is time to pause and reflect."

Followers are nice to have on social media, sure. But keep in mind that having social media 'followers' doesn't make you a leader—far from it. Having followers on social media doesn't make you a leader any more than having people to talk to make you a speaker.

I once saw a meme on Facebook that said: *"Being popular in Facebook is like sitting at the cool table in a mental hospital."*

That's true enough.

Another one I like said: *"Being famous on Facebook is like being rich at Monopoly."*

Indeed, the social media environment has effectively obliterated the once relevant assertion that "leadership is influence."

Everything Rises and Falls on… Social Media?

"Everything rises and falls on leadership" is yet another insightful quote by leadership teacher John C. Maxwell. It has been observable on many levels and cross-culturally in much of history.

Today, however, as we have seen, there are new ways to influence others that are redefining influence, success, leadership, *and especially followers*. There are things other than leadership that make people, ideas, or things rise and fall. Undoubtedly, social media is leading the way in these advancements.

Michael Hyatt, a leader in the fields of personal development and marketing, said:

"Social media is the greatest leadership tool ever invented. It gives you the opportunity to amplify your voice, extend your influence, and create a tribe of passionate followers who want to hear from you."

Indeed, social media has revolutionized pretty much everything in our worldwide marketplace. Ever since its curious beginning, it has redefined how we interact, connect, and influence one another; some of it for the better, some of it obviously for the worse.

So, let's examine both the positive and negative sides, shall we?

The Positive: Social media has given people everywhere a low-cost platform to further their influence and gather a significant following.

Many would-be leaders and influencers would probably not have had a snowball's chance in hell before the rise of social media and its amazing reach. So, for many who may not have much capital for a startup, it has proven a great opportunity to further themselves, their product, their service, or their business in the ever-growing worldwide marketplace, provided, of course, that they are willing, able, and smart enough to leverage it the right way.

So, social media offers a BIG advantage for the individual with a BIG idea and a small pocketbook. But let's also consider…

The Negative: For some other individuals, social media has only alienated them in the immense worldwide web marketplace.

The valuable contributions of many have been lost in the overwhelming noise of social media worldwide.

For instance, those who are not very adept (techy) with online marketing, blogging, online business building, online networking, video marketing, and online sales platforms have found themselves at a loss before the complexity of it all.

Some of you would argue that if they were genuine leaders, they would find a way to keep up with the upward trend of social media marketing. You might say that their problem is not a lack of resources, but a lack of resourcefulness. It's a valid point.

Nonetheless, I would argue that some of these people have great products and/or services and are left in the dust for lack of tech-savvy skills and perhaps financial leverage. Sadly, not all voices can or will be heard, even with the advantage of social media. Sadder still is that not all voices heard are good or useful for our civilization. Whether we will admit it or not, the loss of these worthy voices becomes, in the end, our loss as a society as well.

Here are some further observations regarding these trends.

We find ourselves bombarded with a slew of voices, leaders, influencers and entrepreneurs, whose products or services may or may not be that great because they were able to leverage social media in a BIG way.

These become the voices we hear the most and the movers and shakers of, dare I say it, the world we live in. Clearly, some of these voices are leading us in questionable directions.

Through their massive influence, they weave the fabric of society and many of them have values, philosophies, and opinions that either dumb us down or sell us straight out lies.

Late rock singer Jim Morrison said it best: *"Whoever controls the media controls the mind."*

Unfortunately, there are numerous virtuous individuals with revolutionary ideas who couldn't effectively utilize social media due to various reasons like lacking tech skills, charisma, resources, or finances. These individuals may have had a positive influence on our society, but their voices will go unheard. They were drowned out.

The world wide web is a jungle. In a jungle, it all hinges on survival of the fittest. It's about the most adaptive—not about the truest, noblest, or even the best. And in the social media jungle, it's the one with the best jingle that gets noticed.

Indeed, *everything rises and falls on social media.*

Just like Jesus warned His generation about the Pharisees' leaven, we need to be cautious about the leaven of influence of social media.

Position Yourself

Despite the many ills of social media, one thing is for sure: it is the place where much of the world's influence is generated—the good, the bad, and the ugly.

As a leader, you will either run with it, and possibly gain followers (i.e. customers, listeners, impact, and/or income) in the process, or choose to ignore it and be ignored.

May this serve as a word of caution: Ignore social media and, I don't care how good, capable, or smart you are, you will be ignored. It's that simple.

Like it or not, social media is where people gather to discuss ideas, exchange services, and offer products. In other words, it's where people go to exert their… *influence.*

Regardless of your talent in this area, staying away from social media is no longer an option for mission-driven individuals.

Whether you are a leader in the field of pie-making, chemistry, or mass media marketing, this is where you need to position yourself if you are going to have an impact—whether negligible or significant. This is just where we are as a society. As leaders, we need to be adaptive to the reality that surrounds us in order to be relevant to the surrounding culture.

Social media is the best opportunity you and I have to position ourselves if we are willing to bend ourselves to learning its basics and its intricacies. It is a great way to be heard in an increasingly noisy world. It is a tool. It gives a chance to the little guy, the underdog, and yes, to *the leaders without followers* to get noticed and possibly even get out of their rut.

Are You Visible Enough?

There's no denying that taking advantage of social media as a tool can significantly expand your reach.

Imagine a situation where two men run a business selling lawnmowers.

Guy number 1: Has a distaste for social media. Has a corner shop in his town of 50,000 people, doesn't have a website, doesn't sell online, and barely advertises other than through traditional means (word-of-mouth, flyers, newspapers, etc.). Well, his reach and visibility will be roughly… 50,000 people. He still lives and makes business within the local geographical limits of his town, and in the 1980s.

Guy number 2: Also has a distaste for social media. But, unlike guy number 1, he understands its necessity for business. He has a corner shop in his town of 50,000 people. But he also has a website. He sells lawnmowers, lawnmower parts and equipment online. He has a weekly blog about lawn care and gardening. He does YouTube videos about lawnmower repairs, and he posts ads on Google and Facebook about his online store.

Interestingly, guy number 2's reach is now expansive. It far exceeds his town limits and, as a result, it can significantly grow his business and income! In fact, it can make him *a leader in the field of lawn care and gardening!* He gets it. He lives *in the now*.

Guy number 2 simply decided to adapt to our modern reality to extend his reach. He understands that the more visibility he has (i.e. eyeballs on him, his products, his services), the better the chance of selling more lawnmowers. He understands that the web and social media can provide him with that platform—for a relatively small investment.

The same goes for any other types of business or service promoted online.

Renowned marketing expert Gary Vaynerchuk, said the following about the reality of social media marketing and positioning:

"99% of people don't market in the year that we are actually living in."

What he meant by that is fairly obvious. Too many ignore *new* methods and trends and still advertise through quasi-obsolete means, i.e. word of mouth, radio, and newspapers. While these can still be leveraged for growth, they offer a vastly inferior reach.

Vaynerchuk also gave a tongue-in-cheek definition of social media for those who prefer watching it from the sidelines:

"So-cial Me-dia: noun. A term to describe the current state of the internet and the place where the consumer's attention is."

Now, if you are a leader, with or without followers, who is content and happy with his current results, good for you. Keep going and doing whatever it is you've been doing.

If, however, you're dissatisfied with your current outcome (income, impact, influence) and haven't attempted to reach more people through social media, it's time to stop complaining and *start taking action*. But as you do, here are some...

Pitfalls to Avoid

Being a leader on social media presents various challenges due to its diverse interactions and complexities. As your followers, influence, and success increase, remember to avoid common pitfalls.

Here are the most notable…

1. **Pride:** An inflated number of likes, shares, and followers can gradually lead even the best of us down a path where humility will take a back seat.

   One of my friends once posted the following observation on Facebook:

   "The number of friends/followers we have is insignificant. Jesus only had 12 followers, and he turned the world upside down. Fun fact: 63% of your followers and mine are inactive or scam accounts. There really isn't that much to boast about. So, people who are 'follower hungry' need to let go of numeracy and embrace humility."

   Indeed, no matter how successful you get, stay humble, my friend. And remember, humility is not thinking less or yourself, but thinking of yourself less. Which brings me to the next point.

2. **Self-Centeredness:** If not careful, social media influence can make someone become a glutton for attention, money, or both. When this happens, your focus goes from caring for others to caring for yourself. Remember, as a leader, it's not about you. It never was. If you don't get this, go back and re-read chapters 3 until it sinks in.

3. **Distraction:** While we must be careful not to become attention-seeking, we must also be mindful that other people usually are, and that social media itself is an attention thief. These platforms are tailor-made to keep you enthralled and distracted. People's comments, their posts, videos, ads, memes, the list of stuff that can steal your focus is long. So, be vigilant. You don't want to find out you lost an hour because you were just checking in for two minutes.

The example of Nehemiah, in the Bible, comes to mind when talking about having an unwavering focus. In Nehemiah 6:1-4, we read the following:

"Now when Sanballat and Tobiah and Geshem the Arab and the rest of our enemies heard that I had built the wall and that there was no breach left in it (although up to that time I had not set up the doors in the gates), Sanballat and Geshem sent to me, saying, "Come and let us meet together at Hakkephirim in the plain of Ono." But they intended to do me harm. And I sent messengers to them, saying, "I am doing a great work and I cannot come down. Why should the work stop while I leave it and come down to you?" And they sent to me four times in this way, and I answered them in the same manner." (ESV)

I'm doing a great work; I can't come down. Nehemiah's answer is epic! *"I am doing a great work and I cannot come down. Why should the work stop while I leave it and come down to you?"*

Four times they came to veer him off his work, and four times he gave the same reply.

Well, you too have a great work to do. Once you discover and embrace it, make sure you stay on track, as others may not have much regard for your determination and excitement, whether on social media or in your everyday life.

4. **Groupthink:** In the digital landscape, we all face the insidious risk of *groupthink*.

The Merriam-Webster dictionary defines *groupthink* this way:

"A pattern of thought characterized by self-deception, forced manufacture of consent, and conformity to group values and ethics."

So, basically, groupthink is a more socially accepted form of peer-pressure. The phenomenon occurs when the desire for group harmony and consensus, whether in decision-making or opinion-forming, overrides realistic evaluation of alternatives, leading to poorer decisions, opinions, and ultimately, behaviors.

Social media platforms, equipped with algorithms and, for the most part, a distinct leftist agenda, intensify this issue by forming echo chambers. These are digital spaces where similar opinions are promoted, while dissenting voices are made less visible, censored even; reinforcing a narrow and accepted view of reality.

As leaders, understanding how groupthink operates though any media, social or otherwise, is crucial. By prioritizing critical thinking for yourself and challenging the groupthink consensus, you can nurture a philosophy where your opinions will be your own; born from reason, reflection, virtue, prayer, and research, rather than stifled by group conformity.

5. **Deceit:** One of the greatest pitfalls of social media is the temptation to be disingenuous or fake. Deceit is rampant on social media. People want to appear their best. They wish to prove they are "living their best life." As a result, many like to show off. Many will apply filters to change their appearance, or post pics of their outings to expensive restaurants, or of their trips to exotic places. After all, when your follower list grows past the thousands, many eyes are on you, right? Now, don't get me wrong, there's nothing wrong with sharing some significant moments in your life and trying to make a good impression. But through it all, remain genuine. Being truthful has become a colossal task for most people on social media nowadays, including myself.

With that said, the widespread appreciation for genuineness and transparency on social media might surprise you.

At some point in 2022, we were going through a severe financial drought. We were facing a critical situation with no food, mortgage concerns, and the looming possibility of losing our house and becoming homeless. I felt compelled to make difficult decisions. After prayerful consideration, I took to

Facebook to share my predicament and ask my virtual friends for some assistance.

At the time, I had around 1000+ connections. I figured some of them might be able to spare a few bucks to help a "friend" in need. So, as honestly as I could, I crafted a candid Facebook post, describing the details of my predicament.

Well, my candidness and authenticity paid off—*literally*. People were beyond generous! The donations poured in through PayPal and topped $3000! We were incredibly grateful for the generosity landslide that came just when we needed it.

I'll never forget that miraculous day, and neither will my wife and children. I still get teary-eyed when I think about it.

In hindsight, however, was it easy to be honest and transparent to that degree? Heck, no!

As a responsible man, I take pride in providing for my family. I always have. So, at the time, admitting I was failing as a provider was gut-wrenching. But, in retrospect, it was more than worth it. It also showed me who recognized and valued my contributions as an author, teacher, and podcaster. It showed me that I had, yes, friends, but also *followers,* even secret ones, who appreciated me as a person and gave liberally.

Considering The Darker Side of the Age of Influence

So far in this chapter, I have argued that there are countless benefits for you as a leader to leverage social media in order to grow your influence further and, hopefully, garner some levels of success as a leader.

Also, in the previous chapter, we thoroughly examined the differences between genuine leadership and mere influence. We considered how influence can be *good* or *bad*, while leadership can only be called such if it is positive.

As we move further along, however, I feel it is necessary to address the downright *ugly side* that can come about through social media, or by the unbridled desire to become an influencer—which can creep up on the more naïve would-be leaders. In the upcoming chapter, we will further explore this very concerning topic.

CHAPTER 8

The Perils of Narcissism

"Half the harm that is done in this world is due to people who want to feel important. They don't mean to do harm, but the harm [that they cause] does not interest them. Or they do not see it, or they justify it because they are absorbed in the endless struggle to think well of themselves."

~T. S. Eliot

Successful psychologist, author, and YouTuber, Dr. Ramani Durvasula rightfully observed that, *"Social media is just a tool, not an identity. The number of your likes and followers shouldn't define who you truly are."*

Her reflection echoes that of Epictetus, the Greek philosopher, who said, *"When someone is properly grounded in life, they shouldn't have to look outside themselves for approval."*

The subtlety of how one can go from simply seeking more attention, exposure, expansion, or sales, to wanting some recognition, to craving attention, and to finally becoming a self-obsessed individual is extremely gradual and insidious. But the bottom line is that it always begins with someone having some form of *low self-worth*.

You will not likely fall for the seduction of social media hype if you are self-assured, know your worth, and find meaning in your relationships with God, your family, and other stand-up individuals in your circle.

Be mindful, however, that the curated aspect of social media fosters a high degree of self-centeredness and can contribute to the development of narcissistic behaviors as individuals aim to uphold an idealized image.

This understated process can begin with the mere aspiration to make a few sales or connections, engage in some marketing, create a YouTube video, hustle, and/or take some selfies. Soon, however, if your ego is not in check, this can become gradually obsessive and lead into the dark world of self-obsession and narcissistic tendencies. In the most severe cases, it has the potential to progress into a full-blown narcissistic behavior.

At this point, I feel it is important to establish a distinction between narcissism and self-esteem, which is a healthy psychological trait to possess. Self-esteem, characterized as the overall self-assessment of one's worth and capacity, shares common ground with narcissism. However, recent data supports the idea that narcissism and self-esteem can differ widely in various aspects. Both narcissism and high self-esteem involve positive self-evaluations, but narcissism adds entitlement, exploitation, superiority, and negative views of others, while high self-esteem doesn't necessarily.

As leaders, we should work towards developing a healthy level of self-confidence. Mentally healthy and mature individuals should possess the ability to assess their strengths and weaknesses effectively.

To that end, I believe we should apply the following advice from the apostle Paul:

"For I say, through the grace given to me, to everyone who is among you, not to think of himself more highly than he ought to think, but to think soberly, as God has dealt to each one a measure of faith." ~Romans 12:3, NKJV

Who Was Narcissus?

In Greek mythology, Narcissus was a beautiful youth who became the symbol of self-love and vanity. The most well-known version of the Narcissus myth comes from Ovid's *Metamorphoses*.

According to the myth, Narcissus was exceptionally handsome, and many fell in love with him, including the nymph, Echo. However, Narcissus rejected all romantic advances. One day, as he was wandering in the woods, he encountered a pool of water. When he looked into the water, he saw his own reflection and fell deeply in love with his own image. Unable to tear himself away, Narcissus eventually died by the side of the pool. In some versions of the myth, he transforms into a flower, the narcissus or daffodil.

The term "narcissism" is thus derived from this Greek myth and used to describe an excessive love for oneself, self-centeredness, and an obsession with one's own appearance or abilities.

Does Social Media Facilitate the Spread of Narcissism?

In recent years, we have seen a multiplication of internet content, i.e. blogs, videos, and social media posts addressing narcissism, or the plight of those who have been in a relationship, whether romantic, parental, or fraternal with narcissists. Psychologists, coaches, and therapists have all observed an increase in this personality disorder, as well as the resulting emotional harm and an influx of individuals seeking help. As a result, many clinical experts have gone on to address this topic and worrisome trend head on. This, I believe, is no mere coincidence.

Since the creation of Facebook, back in 2004, social media has basically taken over the digital world, with an estimated 5 billion users two decades later. Considering how the world's population is a little over 8 billion, this statistic is simply *staggering*.

The multiplication of social media *platforms* has further added, I believe, to the rising tide of narcissism. Social media users generate their own content. Many use it mostly for *self-promotion*, *self-glorification*, to look important, to show popularity, and to gain attention. Recent research indicates that today's youth are exhibiting higher levels of narcissism than ever. According to the magazine *Psychology Today*, it is believed that over 10% of individuals in their 20s suffer from subclinical narcissism. All signs point to social media as an undeniably parallel contributing factor.

As a result, there is legitimate concern right now from mental health professionals about how the west is undergoing a narcissism epidemic. I believe this phenomenon is no stranger to the popularity and widespread use of social media. The two seem to have grown exponentially alongside one another in the last couple of decades.

While at first glance social media may appear harmless for connecting with others, it provides a perfect platform for those with narcissistic tendencies to showcase their fabricated identities and ruthlessly exploit the "fake it till you make it" strategy to achieve their objectives. Like moths to a streetlight, dishonest narcissists flock to social media.

According to Dr. Ramani Durvasula, whose clinical specialty is *narcissistic personality disorder* (NPD), today's widespread availability of this tool allows narcissists to receive validation from a global audience, not just their immediate circle. It has completely transformed the concept of narcissistic supply. In our age of influence, narcissists desire more attention than previous generations, and social media provides them with the perfect outlet.

When not careful, the pursuit of constant validation can foster narcissistic tendencies, as individuals prioritize self-image over genuine connections.

Dear leader, don't let this become you. Avoid succumbing to behaviors that can harm you just because of the stigma attached to having a small following.

Eight Defining Traits of a Narcissist

In psychology, *narcissistic personality disorder* is a mental health condition characterized by a pervasive pattern of grandiosity, a need for admiration, and a lack of empathy for others. It falls under the category of personality disorders in the *Diagnostic and Statistical Manual of Mental Disorders* (DSM-5), which is a widely used manual for diagnosing mental health conditions. Here are the key features of *narcissistic personality disorder*:

1. **Grandiosity:** A person with NPD often has an exaggerated sense of self-importance. They may exaggerate achievements and talents, expecting to be recognized as superior without commensurate achievements.

2. **Fantasy of Unlimited Success, Power, Brilliance, or Beauty:** Individuals with NPD may harbor fantasies of unlimited success, power, brilliance, or beauty. They often believe they are special and/or unique and should associate with high-status individuals or institutions.

3. **Need for Excessive Admiration:** People with NPD have an excessive need for admiration and validation. They may seek constant attention, praise, and reassurance from others.

4. **Sense of Entitlement:** Individuals with NPD often have an unreasonable expectation of especially favorable treatment or automatic compliance with their

expectations. They may take advantage of others to achieve their own goals.

5. **Interpersonally Exploitative:** People with NPD may exploit others to achieve their own ends. This can manifest in various forms, such as taking advantage of others to get what they want or manipulating situations to their advantage.

6. **Lack of Empathy:** A notable characteristic of NPD is a lack of empathy. Individuals with this disorder may be unwilling or unable to recognize or identify with the feelings and needs of others.

7. **Envy or Belief that Others are Envious:** Individuals with NPD often believe that others are envious of them, and at the same time, they may be envious of others.

8. **Arrogant or Haughty Behaviors or Attitudes:** People with NPD may display arrogant attitudes or behaviors, coming across as condescending and disdainful of others.

It's important to note that while some level of narcissistic traits or behavior may be present in most of us at times, *narcissistic personality disorder* however, involves a *persistent pattern* of these traits that significantly impairs social, occupational, or other areas of functioning.

As a disclaimer, I would also add that this book is not to be used as a diagnosis tool. Diagnosis and treatment of NPD should be conducted by a mental health professional (also see the disclaimer page at the beginning of this book).

The Four Types of Narcissists

According to mental health professionals, narcissists can be categorized into four different types:

1. Grandiose narcissists are characterized by their egotism, arrogance, and desire for power and attention.

2. Covert or vulnerable narcissists always shift blame onto the world for not recognizing their greatness.

3. Communal narcissists exhibit self-praise for their charitable acts, yet lack genuine empathy for those they assist.

4. Malignant narcissists are the immoral of society. These individuals have no conscience, as they can steal, lie, and cheat without caring about the pain they inflict on others. They often exhibit distinct psychopathic traits. Sadly, they also connivingly climb their way to the top of the power structure.

But experts have now identified a *new breed* of narcissist, prevalent and spreading exponentially on social media…

The Digital Narcissist

The phenomena of online narcissistic behavior have risen to such heights that psychologists had to come up with a new term to define narcissistic behavior that is tied to social media use. It is now referred to as *digital narcissism*.

Here is its definition.

digital narcissism: *Excessive social media usage to seek approval and admiration by indulging in exhibitionism, ostentation,* *and self-inflation, which involves taking many selfies, sharing an excessive number of personal moments, and/or inappropriate self-disclosure.*

While social media platforms connect people, they can also be a breeding ground for narcissism, with influencers often prioritizing self-promotion over authentic engagement.

Digital narcissists often exhibit the combined traits of the grandiose narcissists and communal narcissists. Their inflated ego seeks the limelight of a social media presence via a phone camera wherever they go. They are egotists with a tremendously exaggerated need for attention and some of them even engage in "live" charitable acts while having no genuine empathy for those they help.

And yet, despite some of these people being, unbeknownst to most, some of the most despicable human beings on the planet, they often have millions of followers who admire them and aspire to be like them.

What a shame.

Narcissists and the Dunning-Kruger Effect

The Dunning–Kruger Effect, a cognitive bias prevalent in narcissists, occurs when individuals with limited competence mistakenly believe they are highly skilled in a specific area. Researchers of this phenomenon also noted the opposite effect for high performers, whose tendency is to underestimate their skills.

Consequently, by way of the Dunning-Kruger Effect, highly skilled individuals assume that things they find easy are also easy for others, while the unskilled are so incompetent that they can't recognize their own inanity.

The convergence of many online narcissist influencers and the Dunning-Kruger Effect creates an intriguing intersection where self-centeredness meets overconfidence, often resulting in such crass incompetence.

Digital narcissists, some observe, exude the confidence of skilled individuals, despite lacking the necessary competence. Digital narcissism, therefore, is a camouflage system used in plain sight by online influencers who skillfully disguise themselves as competent and confident individuals, successfully baiting others hook, line, and sinker.

As previously noted, an exaggerated sense of self-importance and an insatiable need for admiration characterizes narcissist influencers. Therefore, they thrive in the digital age of social media. Propelled by their self-assuredness, no matter how misled or delusional, with the added constant validation from their hordes of devoted followers, they very often fall prey to the Dunning-Kruger Effect.

Although this phenomenon is now widespread, it is nothing new. Back in the 16th century, Erasmus, a Dutch theologian, noticed this dire problem, penning these sobering words:

"The less talent they have, the more pride, vanity, and arrogance they have. All these fools, however, find other fools who applaud them."

Both influencers and their audiences face tangible consequences due to the toxic combination of blind leaders and their followers.

On one hand, unaccountable narcissistic influencers may spread misinformation, outright lies, or present themselves as experts in areas where they lack genuine proficiency—thus deceiving, defrauding, and potentially hurting many. As a result, it is not uncommon for some of these individuals to find themselves tangled in some legal problems related to fraud.

On the other hand, naïve audiences, swayed by the influencers' charisma and confidence, may be susceptible to their lethal influence without proper scrutiny. It functions, in effect, much like a cult, although to an arguably less harmful degree.

Often, and additionally, the influencer not only fakes competence, but virtue as well. It is easy to see why this, too, is problematic. The reason is self-evident, so there is no need for further elaboration on this point.

The Clueless Masses Enabling Narcissistic "Leaders"

Our western society's failure to discriminate between *wholesome leadership, influence, and narcissism* has only further contributed to the spread of narcissistic leaders being promoted to top positions of influence—whether in person or online.

Experts estimate that around 3% of any given population consists of malignant narcissists. Nevertheless, we now have to deal with a high percentage of narcissists, psychopaths, and sociopaths in elevated positions in our organizations, city councils, levels of government, schools, and yes, in our churches as well.

Due to their cunning, ruthless, and deceptive methods for advancement, their percentage in those desirable positions well exceeds 3%. Surely, the naivete of the populace has become the narcissist's greatest enabler. The sheep are clueless, it seems, so the wolves among them are rampant. They feed mercilessly, dressed in fluffy white wool, mostly unrecognized by the oblivious masses.

This phenomenon has spawned due to many factors. Firstly, because of how people's morals have been sliding downhill in the last few decades, sure. But also because of who our society embraces as their heroes. The adage is true that says, *"Show me your heroes and I will tell you who you are."*

I encourage you to partake in an interesting exercise. Google the following: top influencers of ______ (insert current year).

As you consider the list that will appear before you, it is plain to see that many (not all) of these people's contributions to humanity oscillate between small to insignificant. While they are celebrated as "leaders", "influencers", or people of genuine competence, most contribute little in reality. This is as much our fault as a society for enabling their pedestal as it is theirs for standing on it and soaking it all in.

The Modern Pied Pipers of Social Media

The medieval tale of the Pied Piper of Hamelin, who lured away an entire town's children with his magical flute, provides a stark metaphor for today's online leaders and influencers. The term "pied piper" has become an allegory for a person who attracts a following through charisma or false promises. Indeed, modern Pipers use social media platforms and persuasive rhetoric not unlike the Piper's flute, drawing followers into a mesmerizing but dangerous dance.

In this age of influence, charisma has become a powerful and deceptive tool for manipulation. Online leaders and influencers craft idealized selves, presenting an allure that is often more enchanting than genuine. This magnetic charm captivates audiences, making it challenging to differentiate between authentic and virtuous leadership and mere spectacle.

Like the streets of Hamelin filled with enchanted tunes, the social media environment creates these echo chambers that amplify specific and deceitful messages lulling the masses to undiscerning slumber.

The cost of succumbing to these captivating figures is profound as we see its disheartening effects even now.

In the long term, society risks losing its capacity for critical analysis, being constantly swayed by sensationalist rhetoric that prioritizes emotionalism over empirical truth. As many find themselves entranced by these modern Pipers, remaining vigilant becomes more necessary than ever. Seeking and appointing leaders who offer substance, integrity, and genuine insight over superficial charm is also proving crucially important.

Gradual Social Conditioning

Two main factors contribute to people's struggle in distinguishing between agenda-driven narcissists and genuinely good individuals.

1. **Moral decline.** As a society, our moral rectitude and virtues have declined significantly over the last generations. This has resulted in a confused perception, blurring our judgement of what is good and what is evil. Consequently, our tolerance for evil has increased. This isn't haphazard. It is contrived. Back in 1984, KGB defector Yuri Bezmenov was interviewed and explained KGB (Soviet) Manipulation of U.S. public opinions in a push to implement socialist/communist philosophy in America. He described the long-term goal of ideologically subverting the U.S. as *"a great brainwashing"* comprised of four basic stages. The first stage, and most important, he said, is called *"demoralization,"* (to be

understood as the gradual abolishment of morals) which would take about 20 years to achieve. According to Bezmenov, the demoralization process, once achieved, is irreversible. And we are way past the 20-year mark since its inception. You can watch this chilling interview here: https://www.youtube.com/watch?v=yErKTVdETpw

2. **Media propaganda.** The media, predominantly owned and controlled by such individuals, now plays a bigger role in conditioning us to admire or honor sick and twisted individuals. For instance, we went from merely tolerating homosexuality in the 70s and 80s to celebrating transgendered teachers in our schools today. To justify this, experts have also been medicalizing every form of sin or vice, ranging from alcoholism to even pedophilia.

Although I detest it and wish to expose it, I am still fascinated by this gradual social conditioning. As an 80s child, I grew up witnessing its unfolding. In the 70s and 80s, for instance, villains on TV and in movies were clearly depicted as evil, psychotic, and unsympathetic—especially in cartoons. From Bluto in Popeye, to General Zod in Superman II, to Skeletor in He-Man, to Megatron in Transformers; these villains were completely devoid of any redeeming qualities. They were clearly 100% evil, so we never cheered for any of them to win— well, at least I didn't.

But then, in the late 70s, Star Wars was released to the big screen, and a cultural phenomenon was born. The revolutionary 70s movie series brought to the big screen one of its greatest villains to date: Darth Vader.

But Vader wasn't your typical unidimensional psycho who wanted to rule the galaxy. He was also a father, and a man who had suffered much, being gradually won over to the dark side — despite his better intentions. The complexity of the character was clear and a new concept brought to the forefront for all to witness: the villain we felt sympathy for.

Ever since then, Darth Vader has been used as a model character for many other villains we tend to sympathize with in entertainment: Thanos, Maleficent, Black Adam, The Joker, to name just a few.

Although TV is just one aspect of this wide-ranging subversion strategy, I think it has significantly influenced our collective generational mindset, making us sympathize with the real-life villains around us. The naivete of the masses allows narcissists and psychopaths to thrive, turning them into influential and admired individuals—ultimately transforming them into celebrities. As a consequence of this gradual and subtle brainwashing, many of these dishonest individuals are now being given respected positions and advancements in our corporations, city councils, and churches.

When Influence Goes Too Far

A narcissist's tools reach far beyond mere influence and have a significant effect. To achieve their objectives, narcissists resort to manipulation tactics, and sometimes, even delve into witchcraft.

So, what is the difference between influence and manipulation?

Leaders must acknowledge the danger of their influence crossing into manipulation by intentionally exploiting the feelings and emotions of others. We need to properly evaluate *why* we are doing something and what we hope to achieve. When our motivations are self-centered or our desired outcomes are selfish, we end up manipulating instead of influencing.

Douglas McArthur, the famous U.S. Army General, said, *"A true leader has the confidence to stand alone, the courage to make tough decisions, and the compassion to listen to the needs of others. He does not set out to be a leader, but becomes one by the quality of his actions and the integrity of his intent."*

The fundamental difference between manipulation and influence, therefore, is *intent*.

As a leader, does your intent align with principles of honesty, integrity, and mutual benefit? If you are honest in your dealings with others and focus on mutual benefit, you can be assured of effective influence.

In contrast, manipulation involves using psychological force or coercion to make someone do something that only benefits the manipulator. Webster's defines it this way: to control or play upon by artful, unfair, or insidious means especially to one's own advantage.

But what happens when manipulation goes too far? When a narcissist's motives, words, and actions go beyond mere manipulation, they can end up engaging in straight out witchcraft. While you may find this assertion to be exaggerated, I can prove it isn't.

Britannica encyclopedia online defines the nature of witchcraft this way: *witchcraft*, traditionally, the exercise or invocation of alleged supernatural powers to control people or events, practices typically involving sorcery or magic.

Utilizing witchcraft is not a big leap for individuals like narcissists or psychopaths, who are comfortable manipulating people for their own gain. In fact, often, it is the next logical step they take—whether knowingly or not. I believe there is a clear correlation between the increasing popularity of crystals, tarot readings, magick, occult, and spells books, and the prevalence of narcissistic behaviors.

The late Derek Prince, who was a renowned and respected deliverance minister, gave the following testimony about how he came about understanding the true nature of witchcraft in his early ministry years. His insight serves as a powerful warning for any of us who seek to influence others:

"I was a pretty orthodox Pentecostal at that time [in his earlier days of doing deliverance], and I am still a Pentecostal, but maybe not quite so orthodox, and the people that needed deliverance were somebody like, you know, the pastor's daughter or the deacon's wife or the church soloist. I mean the last people who ought to have needed deliverance. And I really became concerned about this. I said, "God, I do hope I'm not getting into something that's not right. So please," I said, "would You tell me what is witchcraft?" And I believe this is the answer He gave me: "Witchcraft is the attempt to control people and make them do what you want by the use of any spirit which is not the Holy Spirit." And then He said, as a kind of corollary: "If any person has a spirit which he or she uses, it is not the Holy Spirit, because the Holy Spirit is God and no one uses God." I'll say that first part again:

Witchcraft in its essence is the attempt to control people and make them do what you want by the use of any spirit which is not the Holy Spirit."

And then, Mr. Prince added the following bomb:

"And then I saw why the church was full of witchcraft, because there are a lot of people who feel they want people to do something and they use any means they can do to get them to do it. Most of them don't realize what they are doing."

I believe this serves as a dire warning to all leaders reading this book—especially believers.

If you wish to honor God and want to properly influence people, check your intent—and re-check it, again and again. Like David, may you earnestly pray:

"Search me, O God, and know my heart; Try me, and know my anxieties; and see if there is any wicked way in me, and lead me in the way everlasting." ~Psalm 139:23-24, NKJV

A Cautionary Tale

I had an acquaintance who, like myself, was a Christian fringe researcher, an author and a teacher. Throughout the years, he had gained a substantial following on Facebook—well over 30,000 people.

As a thought-leader, he naturally espoused and taught some controversial views on a range of topics. As a result, many people came after him daily to challenge his views, some even posting very derogatory comments on his posts and attacking him directly. This social media friend always engaged with them, attempting to (graciously) argue his points. He often wrote very long rebuttals and posts often well in excess of 1,000 words, to explain or justify his various positions on these various topics.

Considering the amount of energy he must have exerted to write these posts, I often believed he should just avoid interacting with these individuals. I could sense the toll it was taking on his well-being. It visibly caused him much chagrin, distress, and sucked a tremendous amount of his time and energy. He was, in my humble opinion, clearly being lured and ensnared by narcissists.

This went on *for years*. Out of genuine concern, I once reached out to him in a private message, urging him to save his energy and ignore the haters. Whether he never saw my message or chose to disregard it, I'll never know. But he never read my friendly counsel nor replied to it.

Then one day, the Lord gave me a powerful dream in which I saw this man in a dire situation that affected his health. In the dream, he seemed out of breath. He was huffing and puffing, his face was red, and I thought he would have a cardiac arrest. I woke up feeling extremely disturbed by this. Convicted, I contacted him through Messenger once more. This time it was to share the dream I had. Leaving detailed audio messages, I warned him of what I dreamt. I also told him that I believed this meant he had enemies who were pushing him to exhaustion, possibly even sickness. Once more, he never got my message, or chose to ignore it. Truth is, I'll never know.

One year later, I received the terrible news of that friend passing away in a very suspicious and untimely fashion. He was only 52. He was very involved in ministry and quite productive, having written many books. He was married, had a son, many friends, sincere followers, and he was a beloved brother in Christ.

Notwithstanding, he also had many enemies, many of which were mercilessly harassing him on social media. This story serves as a cautionary example, urging you to consider why we must...

Avoid Such People

As we reach the end of this chapter, I wish it to be understood that as you endeavor to embrace *your moral obligation to do remarkable things,* you will probably try to position yourself properly on social media. Subsequently, you will need to manage your time and yourself as you aim to grow your influence the right way, with truth and integrity. The primary concern is to resist the temptations and snares of social media. Make sure to steer clear of being self-absorbed, or even worse, self-obsessed.

Conversely, as you engage further on social media, you will need to avoid those with an inflated sense of importance. Narcissists and haters, which are more and more numerous on social media, can act as vampires. They will suck out your time and energy if you fall for their attention-seeking ploys. Learn to recognize them and avoid them.

And, in case you find yourself offended on social media, forgive and let it go, leaving the negativity behind. Dust off your feet as you move on; lest, as the apostle Paul said, Satan should take advantage of you, *"for we are not ignorant of his devices."* (2 Corinthians 2:11, NIV)

That same apostle Paul also warned of certain behaviors the ungodly will exhibit in the end times, noting:

"But mark this: There will be terrible times in the last days. People will be lovers of themselves, lovers of money, boastful, proud, abusive, disobedient to their parents, ungrateful, unholy, without love, unforgiving, slanderous, without self-control, brutal, not lovers of the good, treacherous, rash, conceited, lovers of pleasure rather than lovers of God—having a form of godliness but denying its power." ~2 Timothy 3:1-5, NIV

This passage ends with the following important admonition, *"Have nothing to do with such people."* v.5

So, not only are we to do everything in our power to stay real, avoiding narcissistic behaviors ourselves, but we are also to avoid interactions with such people. Believe me, this is easier said than done on social media, where they're proliferating like roaches. They'll reach out to you through ads, private messages, engage in your posts—criticize, opine, and argue, pushing your buttons in the process. Remember, these people are referred to as "haters" for a reason.

Dear leader, my advice to you is to be biblical and *avoid such people.*

Balancing the Juggling Act of Social Media

As I urge you to go against the grain of today's popular approach of seeking more followers to fee validated, and as I encourage you to embrace the spirit of leadership in this age of influence, I feel I must also encourage you to adopt a balanced approach when it comes to social media as a whole.

On the one hand, *don't ignore it*. We have seen just how detrimental it can be to your progress and success if you do. Those who disregard this useful digital tool may end up isolated and forgotten, missing out on the chance to grow and create a meaningful impact.

On the other hand, *be wary of its intense pull!* In your quest to grow and establish yourself, whatever your niche is, you may become vulnerable to over-indulging in your social media time, presence, and even influence. If you're not steadfast, the compliments from people can confuse you into thinking you're better than you really are. Similarly, the crowd's often brutal criticism may cause significant psychological anguish if you let it.

As leaders, whatever people say about us and about what we do, we should espouse the proper attitude toward it. In the end, remember; *what other people think of you is none of your business*. And ignoring haters is often the best approach.

In that respect, I would like to end this chapter by sharing quotes from two legendary sports coaches; football coach Lou Holtz, and basketball coach John Wooden.

"You're never as good as everyone tells you when you win, and you're never as bad as they say when you lose." ~Lou Holtz

"Be more concerned with your character than with your reputation. Your character is what you really are, while your reputation is merely what others think you are." ~John Wooden

CHAPTER 9

Your Temperament, Your Strengths, Your Leadership

"Know thyself."

~Socrates

Socrates' timeless dictum, "know thyself," captures a simple yet profound wisdom that remains as relevant today as it was in ancient Greece. As a leader, knowing yourself is foundational for leading a life of purpose and impact.

Self-awareness, a quality that many people lack these days, is a fundamental aspect for leaders as it influences their decisions, behaviors, and interactions.

On the practical side, being aware of your temperament, talents, strengths, and weaknesses empowers you to make sound decisions. In addition, it supports your personal growth and improves your well-being. Self-awareness also contributes to a higher level of emotional intelligence (EQ), a vital trait in personal growth. Leaders who possess self-awareness excel at understanding both their own emotions and those of others, staying one step ahead.

Blaise Pascal, the French mathematician and philosopher, wrote:

"One must know oneself. If this does not serve to discover truth, it at least serves as a rule of life, and there is nothing better."

The importance of self-awareness is amplified in the realm of leadership development, where the stakes are higher than life-as-usual.

Therefore, understanding one's temperament, strengths, limitations, and motivations is crucial to forge ahead effectively on the journey, or to stand alone when faced with adversity—as you no doubt have.

Self-knowledge is also a tremendous asset that helps you stand firm, with your head held high, when people doubt you and turn away from you. Ultimately, the expression of your leadership is intricately tied to your temperament, your inner wiring—who you truly are. Consequently, delving deeper into your true essence empowers you with the insight required to pursue your purpose—for the right people, and in the right manner.

In the following pages, we will delve into factors that shape the truth in our lives and mold our human experiences, with a particular focus on understanding human behavior and its underlying motivations.

Numerous factors contribute to shaping who we are, for better or worse. For instance, why do we express ourselves and/or behave in certain ways? Is it a product of nature or nurture? Environment or upbringing? Let's explore the numerous influences that may have shaped your personality. Factors including…

- Introversion vs. extroversion
- Temperament
- Gender differences
- Birth order
- Mindset
- Intelligence, and more!

This chapter will provide valuable information and insights to enhance your self-knowledge and leadership journey.

Introversion vs. Extroversion

At the outset, let's take a look at two fictional individuals who are both influential leaders in their respective lanes.

1. **Anita**, 28, was raised in a single parent home in a low-income neighborhood, alongside her two younger brothers. She is a very attractive, boisterous, right-brained, extroverted, and intuitive woman who started her own make-up company two years ago. Despite some initial challenges, she now has three employees and is thriving.

2. **John,** 32, was raised in an upper middle-class family as an only child. He has an average appearance. He is a deeply introverted, left brained, low-key man who has been fascinated with computers since he was a youth. A year ago, he developed a new app that is now going viral. He has four employees and is thriving.

Anita specializes in fashion and beauty care, while John specializes in Information Technology (IT). So, both Anita and John are successful leaders in their respective fields. Yet, if you were to survey people who just met both of them at a party and asked them to identify the better leader, who would they probably choose? If asked, they would probably single out extroverted Anita, who is more sociable, assertive, and cheerful, correct? And yet, John and Anita both exhibit a comparable level of *leadership competence* and achieve similar results in their respective areas of expertise.

This example serves to demonstrate how someone's temperament affects their leadership style—and ultimately how they are perceived. For the past fifty years, leadership studies have often and unwittingly linked extroversion to superior leadership skills.

While the qualities that define leadership haven't changed since the dawn of time, what attracts followers has been subject to many fads—some wholesome, some not.

In this age of super-stimulating media, movies, noise, and everything else in between, the marked advantage to attract followers tends to go to the extroverts. Extroverts have a knack for attracting and maintaining attention and are usually more boisterous, energetic, and entertaining—qualities that are valued today. It's part of their strength arsenal.

People who tend to be louder, energetic, charismatic, and exciting are more sought after and have, on average, more followers than those who aren't. So it goes with our western culture. I am not trying to offend here; I am merely stating an *observable fact*.

I, for one, as you might have guessed, am unashamedly an introvert. Although I can be quite expressive and entertaining during a live video or public speaking events, I am still more reserved than a full-on extrovert. Back in our podcasting days, when we were questioning the cause of our lack of followership, Elisabeth would tell me I should be more energetic on camera, thinking this might be one possible cause of our problems. Just for the record, it wasn't.

Also, years ago, I read Susan Cain's excellent book: *Quiet—The Power of Introverts in a World That Can't Stop Talking.* It made me ponder further what makes followers flock to leaders. I found that, evidently, culture and temperament of the leader plays a huge part in determining his followership (or lack thereof).

Here is what Susan Cain observed about the extrovert-led culture we live in:

"Introverts often feel like they have to conform to the extroverted ideal in order to be successful. They may feel pressured to be more outgoing and talkative, even if it goes against their natural

inclinations. This can be exhausting and frustrating, and it can lead to feelings of inadequacy and self-doubt.

But introverts need to remember that there is nothing wrong with being quiet and introspective. They have just as much to offer the world as extroverts. In fact, their unique strengths and perspectives can be invaluable in a world that is increasingly focused on noise and distraction.

So introverts, don't try to change who you are. Embrace your introversion and use your strengths to make a difference in the world."
~Susan Cain

Susan Cain's groundbreaking thesis states that introverted leaders tend to generate superior outcomes compared to extroverted leaders. That the most spectacularly creative people tend to be introverts. And that the most innovative thinking happens alone and not in teams. She also points out that one of the central challenges of any business is to bring out the best in its employees. Yet when it comes to introverts—who make up a third to a half of the workforce—corporate leadership strategy mainly consists of asking them to act like extroverts. This, according to Susan Cain, is a serious waste of talent and energy.

I couldn't agree more. But let's examine this further.

Introverts In an Extroverted Culture

I own a copy of Bartlett's Familiar Quotations in my personal library. It's a book I absolutely adore, and I enjoy flipping through its pages often. To be fair, though, most of its amazing and history-making quotes are found, in my opinion, before the 1950s, and are mostly from intellectuals, academics, and statesmen.

This simple observation brought me to the same conclusion as Susan Cain: Success used to be measured by how deep and far you could think; by how soul-searching you could be; and by how knowledgeable you were. This is NOT to say that people today are not capable of revolutionary thinking and deep pondering. Most thought-leaders I follow and admire are actually *waaaay* smarter than I am. Many are, in fact, extroverts. But I now realize that the public they serve, their followers, are very much into the "entertain me or else" mindset.

When we talk about deep thinkers from history, Jonathan Edwards comes to mind. In the 1700s, he was the puritan preacher who sparked the great awakening, particularly through his sermon *'Sinners in the Hands of an Angry God'* in 1741. The man left an undeniable legacy as a powerful thought leader, both in his day and still today.

Many books have been written about Edwards' life, work, and impact on American history and his influential professional legacy.

Scholar Benjamin B. Warfield, of Princeton, has charted the 1,394 known descendants of Edwards. What he found was an incredible testament to the impactful leadership and legacy of Jonathan Edwards. Of his known descendants, there were:

- 13 college presidents.
- 65 college professors.
- 30 judges.

- 100 lawyers.
- 60 physicians.
- 75 army and navy officers.
- 100 pastors.
- 60 authors of prominence.
- 3 United States senators.
- 80 public servants in other capacities, including governors and ministers to foreign countries, and one Vice-President of the United States.

This attests to Jonathan Edwards' incredible legacy. He was a premier leader in his day—no question. Theologians and many Americans still hold him in high regard as a remarkable thinker, philosopher, and Bible scholar. And yet, when he spoke and preached publicly, what was his style? Was he entertaining? Was he, as so many like to shout in most conferences nowadays, *'so excited to be here'*? Well, no. Not at all. In fact, the majority of his biographers note his complete lack of charisma as a speaker. A biography once compared his style to that of a funeral director. That's not very exciting, is it?

All this to say that if a leader like Edwards was conducting his work today, he might have little to no recognition. Of course, this is only hypothetical. Even so, he probably would end up as, you guessed it, *a leader without followers.*

Why, you ask? Because he was a deep introvert–quite uncomfortable in public settings. Today, if called upon to speak in public, Jonathan Edwards would probably end up being booed off a stage.

Ah, the times, how they have changed!

You see, people today have become so enamored with *the packaging* that they often neglect *the content*. Their desires are for excitement, entertainment, and yes, fluff. And lots of it! The majority of individuals today seek leaders and influencers who can provide entertainment and cater to their innate preferences.

Now, I am not saying that today's leaders shouldn't be engaging or even entertaining. Nope. Not at all. In fact, I believe that if you are put in the spotlight, the greatest sin is to be boring. So, whether I'm speaking on a stage, doing a Facebook live, recording a podcast, or writing, I always strive to be entertaining.

What I am saying is this, though:

- Today's extroverted leaders have an edge in gathering followers.
- Today's followers, because of noisy cultural conditioning, tend to flock to extroverted, expressive, excited, and entertaining leaders.

Are You Not Entertained?

Do you remember the scene in the movie *Gladiator*, where Maximus (played by Russell Crowe), lets out his frustration after a bloody contest (which he won) by looking at the Roman coliseum crowd and angrily shouting out to them:

"Are you not entertained?! […] Are you not entertained?!"

In the movie, Maximus had been a general and great leader in the Roman army. He was a virtuous and moral man. He was visibly annoyed that he now served as an entertainer and slave to a narcissistic and treacherous Roman emperor, and a populace in search of entertainment. It was never his calling. For him, this was a severe demotion.

Similarly, while you must be mindful of your approach and delivery when in public, as a leader, catering to the whims and wants of your followers is not part of your calling—unless you are in the entertainment business, of course.

Followers, as we have observed, can be fickle. Although as a leader of your gift, you must serve it with care, integrity and added value, you must remain true to your calling and to who you are in doing so. Remember, the more you care about what people think, the less you'll do what you are called to do.

Now, if you are an outgoing, energetic, and passionate extrovert—stay true to yourself without changing the quality of your service or product. If, on the other hand, you are a deep thinking, analytical, content creating, highly productive introvert, stay true to that as well.

Can you become more engaging in your rapport with others? Sure. As well you should, too! Furthermore, depending on how shy or avoidant you are, maybe that would be a good idea. Perhaps a Dale Carnegie public speaking course or joining the Toastmasters wouldn't hurt. However, perfecting yourself in that way shouldn't interfere with your main calling, gifting, and purpose—it should complement it.

The most gifted accountant shouldn't have to become the world's most entertaining speaker because he is dull. No offense to you if you're an accountant, by the way.

Henry Ford, the revolutionary automobile maker, had a remarkable understanding of the various shades of leadership and their efficiency. As a gifted leader, Ford was perceptive at recognizing ideas, imagination, and innovation among his staff.

Case in point, there is a powerful story told of Henry Ford that took place during an appraisal of his organization. As the story goes, an efficiency expert who had been assigned to make a report complained about a man sitting in his office with his feet up on his desk. When told the name of that individual by the efficiency expert, Ford's response was, *"That man once had an idea that saved me a million dollars. When he got it, his feet were right where they are now."*

The moral of this story is: Some leaders are at their best when they're alone, sitting quietly, and thinking. Others are at their best when they're on a stage, presenting, or shaking hands with hundreds of people.

Which one are you?

The Problem is Your Mindset. Or is it?

If you have been consuming personal development for a while, as I have, you were probably taught the importance of *mindset* in everything you do.

As it stands, we know and understand that a strong, positive, and determined mindset can indeed get you through many tough patches, in both business and life. This is a most important truth. After all, *"as a man thinketh in his heart, so is he."* ~Proverbs 23:7, KJV

An essential tool for achieving success is maintaining a positive mindset that is growth-oriented.

A growth mindset will make you embrace new challenges in a positive light. Furthermore, when encountering obstacles, it will prompt you to reconsider your approach, and to adapt to change. This, in turn, fosters resilience and enables you to find solutions and get through most challenges.

A negative outlook coupled with a *fixed mindset*, however, will deter your growth, and make you quit when obstacles rise. In the end, it will limit your impact on everything you do. It is not the tool of an efficient leader.

Notwithstanding, have you ever experienced hitting an insurmountable wall despite trying to do things outside your comfort zone with a positive mindset and an eager desire to learn and grow?

I know I have—more times than I care to remember. I know others who have as well. Maybe you have, too.

When such outcomes arise, like failures do, it beckons a time for reflection. It is time to pause and revise our checklist of *do's* and *don'ts*. Most of the time, about ninety-five percent, we come to the realization that it's our own fault. There is something we either did or didn't do that bred this failure. Oftentimes, the answer is, as you probably guessed, an adjustment in mindset.

But what about those times when adjusting your mindset just doesn't fix the problem?

Some would say that doesn't happen. They would say that your faulty mindset is to blame 99% of the time. They might even give you the speech about how people have only two options in life: results or excuses.

Well, I disagree.

Sometimes, (get ready for this bomb)… *it's just not your mindset.*

There, I said it. Yeah, I know some of you needed to hear that. Hey, you're welcome!

But keep reading, there's more.

As I experienced more and more failures in my own life, I started to doubt what I had been taught about the influence of mindset, desire, and determination. Nevertheless, the personal development books that have gained the most popularity consistently emphasize that a strong desire and a determined growth mindset can conquer any barrier. Moreover, they emphasize the concept of your "power within" and how self-doubt is the only barrier. Besides, haven't you heard that failure is not because of a lack of resources, but a lack of resourcefulness, etc.?

It all sounds so good and true, doesn't it?

I will now tell you something that is contrary to what you were probably told time and again. Here goes…

No matter what you have been told (or sold); while it is a tremendous asset for a leader, *a strong mindset isn't an unstoppable force.*

Let me repeat that.

A strong mindset, while effective, isn't an unstoppable force.

And if you believe it is, dear reader, you have bought into a lie. In fact, if you believe that it all hinges on your mindset, you have elevated yourself to a position that you cannot possibly maintain—that of God. And I hate to be the bearer of bad news, but no matter how capable you think you are; you, my friend, are not that powerful.

You see, there are *three main things* that can override the strength of your mindset and determination at any given time, and they are:

1. Your Wiring

2. God

3. Reality

1. **Your wiring:** Your wiring encompasses both God's design for you and the influence of your early life circumstances. It is a complex combination of your genetics, temperament, preferences, abilities, experiences, and set neuro-patterns.

You see, when God made you, He already had a special purpose carved out for you. He thus equipped you with a temperament, skills, talents, and leanings that would help you to fulfill this special work assignment. Whether he made you physically robust, intellectually gifted, a lover of things, or a lover of people; this is all part of your *wiring*.

And your wiring plays a huge part in pre-determining what you will choose to do and how good you will be at it.

For example, someone who loves quietude, is detail-oriented, and prefers things and processes over people, will most likely choose a profession along those lines. Such an individual may choose to become an accountant, bookbinder, or scientist. It's doubtful that you would see someone like that take on the roles of an event organizer, salesman, or public speaker, correct?

On the other hand, those who love action, people, and stimuli might find satisfaction in careers such as event organizing, entertaining, or politics, don't you think?

Within your wiring is found your penchant toward extroversion or introversion.

Here is how we can boil it down:

Introverts are (generally) drained by people and crowds, and energized by projects, things, and tasks that require solitude and attention to detail. Therefore, they tend to be laser-focused, appreciate routine, and don't mind working alone for extended periods.

Extroverts are (generally) energized by people and crowds, but tend to dislike projects, things, and tasks that demand too much attention to detail. They tend to be big picture people who like what is new and enjoy working and relating with people to get things done.

So, what does all this have to do with *mindset* you ask?

Well, have you ever heard the saying, *"Where focus goes, energy flows"*? This is very true. What commands our attention demands our energy. Moreover, humans typically prefer the path of least resistance. We naturally want to preserve our energy. We naturally gravitate towards what we excel at and dislike what we struggle with. So, our wiring will often determine our disposition towards tasks preferred or, on a larger scale, career choices.

Picture a scenario where an introvert agrees to work in a sales position that heavily involves dealing with people. He is likely to be more tired by the end of the day compared to his extroverted counterpart. In fact, he might hate his job for this very reason. Why? Because it demands too much out of him, and because it is too far out of his comfort zone. Introverts have what is called "a social battery". Their social battery charge is basically how much energy they can give to social events or groups—which is usually a fairly limited amount compared to extroverts. When this battery is drained, they are too.

Now, some would argue that if our introverted salesman friend isn't successful at the position, it's because he doesn't have a *growth mindset*. Their argument is that he is resistant to change, personal growth, and learning new skills, including sales. But, in all honesty, is the mindset the root cause of the problem here?

It's funny how we tend to blame the mindset of introverts for more extroverted tasks, but the reverse is rarely the case.

Here is another example to illustrate this point.

Imagine taking the most extroverted person you know and placing them in a well-paying job that demands they work alone, performing repetitive, meticulous tasks, like decorative book-binding. If this individual hated it and decided to quit, would we attribute their dissatisfaction to their mindset, or acknowledge that the job simply wasn't a good fit? Would we suggest they should adopt a more positive outlook and a growth mindset to overcome the job's challenges, or would we agree that this type of work isn't for everyone?

Indeed, we would readily excuse the extrovert over this, wouldn't we?

We can thus conclude that wiring, then, is a highly influential factor in determining success at a given task. You can have all the mindset prowess in the world, but if you're doing something you're not cut out for, it won't make much of a difference in the end. Obviously, then, *mindset isn't enough.*

So, which are you? Do you identify as an introvert, someone who tends to be more introspective and focused on their inner world? Or are you someone who thrives on being around people, outgoing and full of energy — an extrovert?

Nevertheless, before you answer, there is an additional type you need to consider — the ambivert. Ambiverts are a less common personality type, skilled at engaging with others and staying focused on tasks for adequate periods of time.

With that said, it is worth repeating that regardless of the strength of your mindset, if you act outside of your *wiring*, it will deplete your energy much faster and more than usual. Most people cannot operate effectively for very long in areas where their energies are rapidly depleted. It goes too much against the grain of their very nature.

Does this mean that an introvert cannot be, say, a successful public speaker? Or that an extrovert cannot successfully write a book? Of course not! In fact, I know of many who have done just that, overcoming their own shortcomings in the process and achieving great results. What it does mean, however, is that such endeavors outside of one's wiring will require much more time and energy for anyone, and in the end, it may or may not be worth the effort.

It might seem like stating the obvious, but amid prevalent contemporary philosophies such as *"you can do anything you set your mind to"* or *"you can be anything you want,"* it is crucial to acknowledge the limitations of these notions. Such ideas, although beneficial to motivate us, should be embraced within reason—a commodity in short supply these days. As the saying goes, *"Common sense isn't so common."*

There exist two more significant impediments to any individual's endeavors that can lead to failure despite the strength and resilience of their mindset. These are God and reality.

2. **God:** Solomon's wisdom, in Proverbs 19:21, remind us of the sovereignty of God: *"Many are the plans in a person's heart, but it is the Lord's purpose that prevails."* The popular saying, "Man proposes, God disposes," distills the essence of this concept.

The Bible's account of Job serves as a poignant illustration of this concept. Despite his impeccable character, strong leadership, entrepreneurial drive, and evidently, a *strong mindset*; Job faced tremendous trials and major failures.

Although the theological complexities of his story are extensive, the bottom line is that God's will triumphed in Job's life. I'm sure you, too, could pinpoint some instances in your life where it didn't matter how much you wanted it, God had other plans. Right?

Regardless of how this makes you feel at first, remember that in the end, *God will ruin our plans so that our plans don't ruin us.*

3. **Reality:** An apt illustration of how reality can sometimes override mindset is to consider the following fictional scenario: imagine I were aspiring to become a National Football League (NFL) player. Tell me, how does this sound for an NFL prospect: I am (at the time of this writing) fifty years old, roughly out of shape, and standing at an unimpressive height of 5'8". Clearly, no matter how much I want it, how you dress it, how hard I train, or how determined I am, becoming a professional football player at the highest level is not a realistic goal — at all. Regardless of how developed or motivated my mindset is, it cannot change the fixed aspects of height, weight, and age in this scenario. That's my reality. And, granted, sometimes reality does suck. But no matter how much it sucks; we have to take it into account in our life and professional choices.

Jesus likens this to *counting the cost*. In the gospels, He says:

"Which of you, intending to build a tower, does not sit down first and count the cost, whether he has enough to finish it—lest, after he has laid the foundation, and is not able to finish, all who see it begin to mock him, saying, 'This man began to build and was not able to finish'? Or what king, going to make war against another king, does not sit down first and consider whether he is able with ten thousand to meet him who comes against him with twenty thousand? Or else, while the other is still a great way off, he sends a delegation and asks conditions of peace." ~Luke 14:28-32, NKJV

Every pursuit we set our minds to under the sun comes with a price tag. Reality, as disenchanting as it may sometimes be, acts as the yardstick to determine whether the cost is reasonable or too steep. Don't forget that numerous individuals have suffered mental breakdowns and significant financial losses by disregarding the truth and embracing delusions of grandeur regarding the unlimited potential of a strong mindset.

So, be advised, while improving it is wise, *it is not worth losing your mind over your mindset.*

Tell Me Your Temperament and I Will Tell You...

The Greek physician, Hippocrates (c. 460–c. 370 BC), from whose philosophy graduating doctors perform their Hippocratic Oath, contributed a great deal to medicine and also to the field of self-knowledge when he came up with the four basic temperaments over 2,400 years ago.

Hippocrates even incorporated the four temperaments into his medical theories. According to Wikipedia, *the four temperaments* is a theory that suggests that there are four fundamental personality types. They are:

1. **Sanguine (optimistic and social)**

2. **Choleric (driven and short-tempered)**

3. **Melancholic (analytical and quiet)**

4. **Phlegmatic (relaxed and peaceful)**

While the theory of four basic temperaments governing personality types has lost popularity with time, I've found that most people fit into these categories, usually with one dominant and one subordinate temperament.

To this day, I can easily recognize those temperament blends in most people. When you are well versed in the four temperaments theory, it is quite easy to surmise another's type. It can even be fun. Moreover, I have found that the study of personality is a really great way to *know thyself,* as Socrates exhorted.

So here is the lowdown of the four basic temperaments and how they relate in the field of leadership.

Sanguine

The sanguine, often labeled as "super-extroverts," thrive in social settings and are natural salespeople. They excel in outgoing professions like acting, public speaking, and, sure enough, sales. Known for leading with their mouth, they effortlessly command attention, enjoy being the center of attention, and are the life of the party. Their energetic, humorous, and tactile demeanor makes them popular, though their impulsiveness and tendency to say *yes* before thinking things through can be drawbacks. Inactivity often induces stress for these fast-paced individuals, but their high energy and cheerful disposition make them a joy to be around.

Choleric

This temperament is identified as the most "powerful" and most leadership-oriented of the temperaments. The Latin word *cholericus* is where the French word *colérique* comes from, which means *'prone to anger'*.

Cholerics are dynamic individuals, often holding leadership roles due to their strong will and determination. Seeking control over themselves and their environment, they believe they know what's best. While efficient planners with a practical and solution-oriented approach, they can be quite stubborn, even abrasive. Their motto is "do it now," and they excel at getting things done. They appreciate respect and esteem for their contribution.

The choleric and sanguine personalities are both characterized by their outgoing and sociable nature, thriving in social settings and effortlessly standing out in a crowd. Their leadership style is naturally driven, energetic, and people-oriented, exhibiting more extroverted leadership qualities.

Melancholic

The melancholy personality is often considered the richest of all temperaments, but it comes at a significant emotional cost, as history may reveal. These individuals harbor a profound love for others while frequently holding themselves in contempt. For instance, when faced with ten compliments and one criticism, a melancholy individual is more likely to lose sleep over the criticism than be encouraged by the compliments. Deep thinkers and feelers, they tend to focus on the negative aspects of life rather than the positive. Susceptible to melancholy and depression, they experience emotions intensely.

The saying by Horace Walpole sums them up well: *"Life is a comedy for those who think, and a tragedy for those who feel."*

Melancholies stand out as the most dependable among the temperaments, driven by their perfectionist tendencies. Their analytical prowess enables them to skillfully diagnose obstacles and problems, often leading them to resist change. Preferring the status quo, they may appear overly pessimistic in their outlook.

In their life vocations, melancholies might choose challenging paths that involve personal sacrifice, such as becoming doctors or scientists. Their almost manic perfectionism, while a strength, can hinder their decisiveness. Additionally, they tend to harbor dissatisfaction with themselves, which translates into high levels of self-criticism.

Phlegmatic

Individuals with a phlegmatic temperament are characterized as inward, private, thoughtful, reasonable, calm, patient, caring, and tolerant. They cultivate a rich inner life, seek tranquility, and find contentment within themselves. Steadfast and consistent in habits, they prove to be steady and faithful friends. Even tempered, their speech may be slow or appear hesitant. Typically not drawn to leadership roles, the calm and peace-loving phlegmatic prefers a more low-key position within an organization. However, if placed in a leadership role, their sharp minds compensate for their seemingly laid-back demeanor. Many phelgmatics find their niche as scientists, authors, and accountants.

The melancholic and phlegmatic personality types lean towards introversion, manifesting as shy and reserved individuals who may feel anxious in crowds, particularly when singled out. Their low-key leadership style is task-oriented, and they excel in dealing with projects and things rather than with people. Their leadership qualities are characterized by introversion. Nevertheless, when called upon to deal with people, being conscientious, they do it well.

So, did you recognize yourself in those temperaments? Would you be able to pinpoint your dominant and subordinate temperaments?

In my youth, I delved into the study of temperaments and underwent a personality test, revealing a blend of 60 percent melancholy and 40 percent sanguine. This classification resonated deeply with my nature at the time. With the passage of time, however, the negative qualities associated with melancholy have gradually waned. Growing older has brought forth a more upbeat and positive nature, significantly enhancing my relationships and work. As my negative outlook diminished and my self-confidence grew, my sanguine side emerged more prominently.

Sydney J. Harris, an American Journalist, stated that *"Character is something you forge for yourself; temperament is something you are born with and can only slightly modify."*

Research and historical evidence validate this statement. Nevertheless, I have found that personal development, along with the passage of time and life experiences, combined with God's help through willful sanctification, can smooth out the rough edges and bring out the best in anyone. It is important to note that this process also reinforces an individual's personal leadership capabilities.

Birth Order and Leadership

Let's talk about something that can give someone an edge in leading others. Science has revealed that the order in which we are born has a direct correlation with our temperament. Studies also show how this may affect our *leadership ability*. You may have noticed it in your family. It's called *the first-born advantage*.

In the May/June 2011 issue of Psychology Today, the Insights section covered *The Power of Birth Order*. It said:

"Parents tend to pour their resources into the firstborn, ensuring that they have the best in life. Thus their IQ is 3 points higher

than their siblings... Middle born tend to be unbiased and level-headed, leading them to careers that involve negotiation. They are well-suited for positions in management and politics... The last born in families with three children typically are tender and altruistic, perhaps because he or she gets babied."

Dr. Kevin Leman, who studied and taught the impact of birth order for over 35 years and authored *The Birth Order Book* and *The First-Born Advantage*, mentions in his book how first-born children have an advantage in becoming the movers and shakers (leaders) of the world:

"Firstborns were born to win. Clearly the natural movers, shakers, and leaders of this world, they can accomplish anything they set their minds to. They're the high achievers, the benchmark-setters, the business moguls, the concert violinists, the heads of the PTA. But if they're out of balance, they can be overly perfectionistic, driven, and critical. They can become controllers (everything has to go their way) or pleasers (exhausting themselves in meeting the demands of others)."

The responsibility and desire to lead people often befalls those who are first-born. Maybe you're a first-born and you have a proven track-record of leadership skills and tendencies in life—which would only confirm the theory.

Or, maybe you're *not* a first-born, like me. Like all generalized theories, there are always exceptions to be noted.

There are many factors and intricacies which affect your birth-order temperament. According to Dr. Leman, the hook in the theory is the following:

"Just because you're the firstborn child in the family doesn't mean you'll have a firstborn personality. You can be #3 in a group of 4 siblings, and still have a firstborn personality!"

Take me, for example. I have just one older sibling, my sister Carolyn, who is four years older. So, in my case, while I am the *last born*, I am also the *first-born male*. And while I am the baby of the family, I was raised for some part of my early years (from 4 to 6) as an only child by my grandparents.

Also to be considered, the gap in age between my sister and I also played a large part in affecting the way I was treated growing up. As mentioned, while I was the baby of the family, I was *the first-born male*, and my sister was significantly older, which gave my parents a 'breather' between her birth and mine. This caused them to view me more as a second first-born rather than a typical last-born. As a result of this birth-order mash, in some respects, I possess some of the qualities of a first-born—even of an only child. In other respects, however, I definitely show signs of being a last-born. Elisabeth, my wife, who is a typical first-born, would attest to that.

So, maybe you're not a firstborn—like me. Maybe you weren't initially trained or prepared for leadership. Still, do you wonder what your birth order might reveal about you?

If so, provided here are some *general observations* of personality traits and birth order. While these are insightful enough to be shared here, you should also take them with a grain of salt, since, after all, there are many other factors at work here:

First-born tend to:

- Be perfectionists
- Be more conscientious
- Be highly motivated to achieve
- Take leadership roles
- Be more responsible

Middle-born tend to:

- Adapt easily to situations
- Play the role of mediator and prefer compromise to conflict
- Be more rebellious than other siblings
- Be independent
- Be inventive
- Develop skills not shared by other siblings

Last-born tend to:

- Be outgoing
- Be able to charm others
- Be considered spoiled, demanding, or impatient
- Be most financially irresponsible
- Feel inferior to older siblings
- Develop skills that older siblings don't have

Only children tend to:

- Be very responsible
- Be even bigger perfectionist
- Get along better with people older than themselves

It is interesting to note that only children exhibit, in many ways, first-born traits, but magnified.

Male and Female Leadership Expression

Understanding leadership expression also requires us to consider the role of gender and how it shapes our leadership approaches, inclinations, and abilities.

Despite current egalitarian beliefs and trends that sometimes border on folly, I maintain that there are marked differences between men and women. These differences affect how we behave as individuals, but also how our personal leadership is expressed.

Woke and leftist influences in western societies have led to a deliberate attempt to blur the clear distinctions between genders, be it in physical, mental, or psychological aspects. The evident intention to remove the recognition of gender disparities from our shared mindset is clearly excessively egalitarian and too multifaceted to fully explore in this context.

Now, before you jump to any conclusion because of this last statement, let me clarify. I strongly support gender equality for both males and females. But, I think this equality exists in the eyes of God, is relevant to human rights, and serves to uphold the social dignity for individuals of each gender. I do not believe in gender equality when it refers to *wiring, predisposition, capacity, and tendencies*. In short, I believe men and women are wired very differently. For instance, men are capable of doing things that most women can't (and will not) do. Likewise, I believe women are capable of doing things that most men can't (and will not) do.

Furthermore, I consider the blurring of gender lines and identities as part of a harmful and devilish agenda that opposes the cultivation of proper behavior, ethics, and a flourishing society.

Individuals who are only mildly observant can readily discern that gender distinctions are evident, multi-layered, and cannot, nor should not be eliminated through the misuse of egalitarianism. Gender differences must be freely expressed for human survival, prosperity, and the fulfillment of God's plan.

We can therefore identify some general differences in the way both genders express their leadership strengths and natural inclinations. Indeed, men and women perceive the world differently. This is not just due to their genetic and intellectual variances. Gender differences are complex and can even translate into spiritual concepts and reality perceptions. Consequently, men and women's individual leadership styles find their expression in different ways.

Left-Brained Masculine or Right-Brained Feminine?

Studies suggest that cognitive behavior and gender leadership expression are closely linked to the favored brain hemisphere associated with gender. In this section, you'll find graphics that accurately illustrate the cognitive and behavioral tendencies of each hemisphere in relation to gender.

While both genders utilize both sides of their brain, in a very generalized sense, men tend to favor the left hemisphere more, and women the right. The left-brain hemisphere is crucial for rational thinking and logical abilities, including math, spatial perception, and language. Conversely, the right hemisphere of the brain is accountable for artistic pursuits and establishing emotional connections with others. Logical thinking is associated with left brain dominance, while right brain dominance is linked to emotional thinking.

The left hemisphere of the brain is also called the digital brain. It is, generally speaking of course, favored by a higher percentage of men. It is the hemisphere responsible for the following functions:

- Verbal
- Analytical
- Order
- Reading
- Writing
- Computations
- Sequencing
- Logic
- Mathematics
- Thinking in words
- Linear thinking
- Visual based languages such as in mute and deaf people

The right hemisphere of the brain is also called the analog brain. It is, generally speaking, favored by a higher percentage of women. It is the hemisphere responsible for the following functions:

- Creativity
- Imagination
- Intuition
- Holistic thinking
- Arts
- Feelings visualization
- Non-verbal cues
- Rhythm
- Daydreaming
- Emotions

The graphics shared here highlight additional fundamental distinctions between the two hemispheres.

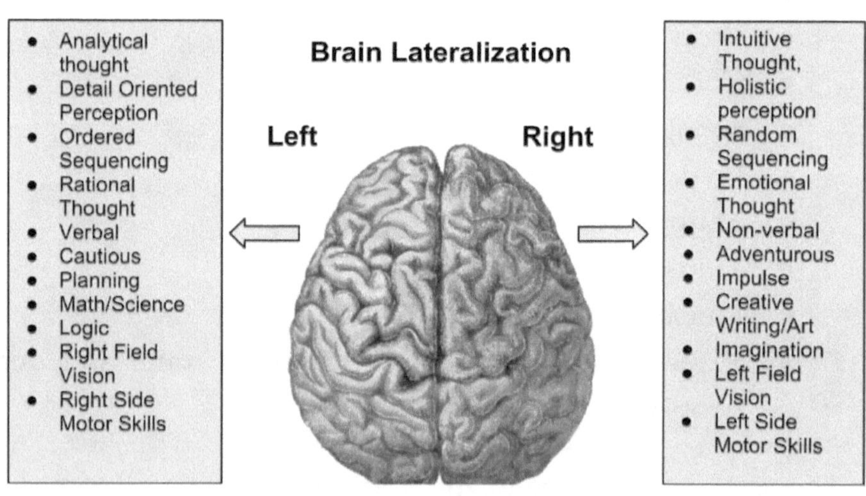

It is interesting to note how, based on this research, men and women exhibit different preferences and behaviors. For instance, women are generally more intuitive, emotional, spiritually inclined, and better at relating with people, while men tend to be better with logic, math, evaluating space, time, and distance and usually show a higher affinity with objects, concepts, and processes than people. One cannot overlook the influence of these natural gender-related inclinations on the formation of one's leadership style.

Other interesting factoids are the following:

- The male brain is 10% larger and has stronger front to back connections, which can result in heightened perception and stronger motor skills.

- The inferior-parietal lobule tends to be larger in men. This part of the brain is linked with mathematical problems, estimating time, and judging speed.

- The female brain's larger corpus callosum enables efficient multitasking and relational navigation by enhancing connections between brain hemispheres.

- Gray matter is more heavily used in the male brain during activities, while the female brain tends to rely more on white matter. This differentiation is thought to clarify why males have a greater ability to concentrate on one task, disregarding their surroundings, whereas women have a knack for shifting between tasks.

The intricate interplay between cognitive behavior and gender has a significant impact on leadership preferences and adoptive styles. Research suggests that men and women, in a broad sense, exhibit distinct cognitive tendencies based on the favored hemisphere of their uniquely wired brains.

Men, as stated, tend to favor the left hemisphere, which is associated with logical thinking, analytical abilities, and proficiency in tasks like mathematics and language. Men, therefore, may excel in direct verbal communication, analytical reasoning, and linear thinking. The left hemisphere's dominance in men may contribute to their inclination towards more structured approaches, order, and logical problem-solving in leadership.

Conversely, women tend to favor the right hemisphere, which is linked to creativity, imagination, holistic thinking, as well as social and emotional connections. Women may excel in areas such as asymmetric reasoning, intuition, and non-verbal cues due to the dominance of the right hemisphere. Their leadership approach usually involves a more intuitive, emotionally attuned approach, valuing creativity, cooperation, and an all-inclusive perspective.

I could list countless other factors that influence how the male and female brain disparities shape their leadership styles, approaches, and preferences. The subject is so extensive, it could be its own book. But I believe the point is made and helps you to understand how this is significant enough to be a determining factor.

How Are You Smart?

Moving forward, let's focus on the connection between intelligence, the brain, and how various types of intelligences greatly influence your leadership expression.

When it comes to understanding yourself better as a leader, the question is not to determine how smart you are, but rather, how you are smart.

Whether we consider the different quantitative intelligences that are being assessed nowadays (IQ, EQ, SQ, Et al.), or the qualitative intelligences, the reality is that your mental penchants greatly influence leadership styles.

IQ, EQ, SQ, & AQ

According to psychologists, there are four main types of *quantitative intelligences*:

1. Intelligence Quotient (IQ)
2. Emotional Quotient (EQ)
3. Social Quotient (SQ)
4. Adversity Quotient (AQ)

1. **Intelligence Quotient (IQ):** This is the measure of your level of comprehension. You need IQ to solve mathematics, memorize things, and recall lessons. Most of us are familiar with this type of assessment, as it is perhaps the most common and observed.

2. **Emotional Quotient (EQ):** EQ was coined in the early 90's by Peter Salovey and John D. Mayer. Not much time passed before Daniel Goleman became familiar with Salovey and Mayer's work, and this ultimately led to his bestselling book, Emotional Intelligence. EQ is the measure of your ability to maintain peace with others, keep to time, be responsible, be honest, respect boundaries, be humble, genuine and considerate.

3. **Social Quotient (SQ):** This is the measure of your ability to build a network of friends and maintain it over a long period of time.

People that have higher EQ and SQ tend to go further in life than those with a high IQ but low EQ and SQ. Most schools capitalize on improving IQ levels while EQ and SQ are played down.

A man of high IQ can end up being employed by a man of high EQ and SQ even though he has an average IQ.

EQ represents your Character, while your SQ represents your Charisma. Give in to habits that will improve these three Qs, especially your EQ and SQ.

Now there is a 4th one, forging a new paradigm:

4. The Adversity Quotient (AQ): The measure of your ability to go through a rough patch in life, and come out of it without losing your mind.

When faced with troubles, AQ determines who will give up, who will abandon their family, and who will consider suicide.

What conclusions can we draw from these different measures of intelligence?

Well, for instance, we can assert that introverts, such as Vincent Van Gogh, Emily Dickinson, and perhaps Nikola Tesla, while clearly brilliant in their own way (IQ & EQ), lacked a significant amount of SQ (Social Quotient). This would serve to explain how they lived much of their lives away from social circles.

Conversely, we can also assert that, generally speaking, extroverts usually score quite high on the SQ scale.

Nine Types of Qualitative Intelligences

"It's not how smart you are that matters, what really counts is how you are smart." ~Howard Gardner

The way we now understand human intelligence is so much more distinctive than back in the day when I.Q. tests were pretty much the only measure we had.

Howard Gardner revolutionized the field of Quantitative Intelligence Studies when his theory (and book) were released in 1983. *Frames of Mind: The Theory of Multiple Intelligences*, was indeed revolutionary in its field.

According to Gardner, *"While we may continue to use the words smart and stupid, and while IQ tests may persist for certain purposes, the monopoly of those who believe in a single general intelligence has come to an end. Brain scientists and geneticists are documenting the incredible differentiation of human capacities, computer programmers are creating systems that are intelligent in different ways, and educators are freshly acknowledging that their students have distinctive strengths and weaknesses."*

Unfortunately, though, even if the theory came out in 1983, society, for the most part, has very slowly and very painfully adapted to the reality of multiple intelligences and types of learning in schools and the workplace. So slowly in fact, that it is severely lagging behind considering this information was brought forth many decades ago.

As the picture above reminds us, this is how most of us (and our kids) are still being treated in most learning institutions. So, guess what kind of grade the elephant will get in the 'Tree Climbing' test above? Probably not a very good one.

But does this make him a failure? No. Does it mean he isn't competent or smart? No. It does, however, mean that he wasn't tested in his area of strength. It also means that he is different from the monkey, the seal, and the penguin. Conversely, the monkey's success in this tree-climbing test doesn't make him smarter or more competent than the other students overall. The test just catered to his own strengths and abilities.

Lack of time and space prevents me from thoroughly examining the subject of multiple intelligences. In my opinion, the list and graphic provided below are self-explanatory when it comes to defining and summing up Howard Gardner's nine types of intelligences.

1. Naturalistic intelligence
2. Musical intelligence
3. Logical–mathematical intelligence
4. Existential intelligence
5. Interpersonal intelligence
6. Linguistic intelligence
7. Bodily–kinaesthetic intelligence
8. Intra–personal intelligence
9. Spatial intelligence

9 Types of Intelligence

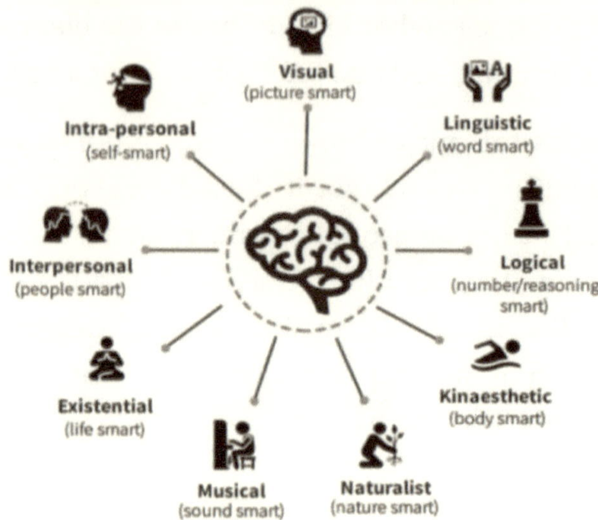

A cursory evaluation of the theory using the above information clearly shows that, for instance, someone who possesses a high degree of interpersonal intelligence (people smarts) would, arguably, fare better in a corporate leadership position than someone who champions one of the other eight intelligences.

This alone further confirms how skewed the present and accepted leadership concept of "everybody can be a leader (of people)" really is.

More Factors to Consider

There are, of course, many more factors that influence each individual's leadership expression. A whole book could be written addressing just those.

Clearly, your natural abilities and spiritual gifts greatly impact your overall life outcomes. Differentiating between those is useful. Natural talents, for instance, are inherently "natural," stemming from the genetic material and intellectual capacity we inherit, which has been passed from one generation to the next. In contrast, spiritual gifts are bestowed directly by the Spirit of God, which is why they are referred to as "gifts." It is the Holy Spirit who orchestrates this, distributing to each individual precisely as He chooses. While natural talents are granted at birth, spiritual gifts are bestowed upon us at the moment of spiritual rebirth—at our new birth. Also note that both the saved and the unsaved possess talents, whereas only the saved are endowed with spiritual gifts.

To truly understand yourself, also, it is crucial to acknowledge and evaluate both your inherent strengths and weaknesses. For instance, although I excel in creativity and intellectual understanding, I struggle greatly with organizational skills. The process of logistics, which involves prioritizing, organizing, and sequencing, is difficult for me. I'm not very proficient at it, to be honest. Others, like my wife Elisabeth, find it effortless and seamless. As a result, I frequently depend on her for issues that require planning and logistics in our everyday household needs.

Your personal love language(s) is another aspect worth investigating. While it may not be a major factor in your leadership journey, it can shape your emotional bond with those closest to you. This is something worth exploring to enhance your self-knowledge and personal growth. The seminal work to consider in that respect is Dr. Gary Chapman's perennial bestseller, *The Five Love Languages*.

Another interesting thing to factor in is the malleability of our brains and our powerful ability to change our thinking, adapt, and shift, through the use of words and thought processes. In short, I'm talking about what is commonly referred to as NLP (Neuro-Linguistic Programming). NLP is particularly valuable in enhancing your personal leadership—the essential skill of leading yourself.

Through consistent NLP, you can better identify and transform limiting beliefs that may be hindering your effectiveness. By replacing these with empowering beliefs, you not only boost your confidence but also enhance your empathy and understanding of others—key traits for any successful leader.

By integrating NLP into your personal development, you can achieve a higher level of self-mastery. This helps you develop a leadership style that is both influential and deeply rooted in an understanding of human behavior and communication. Start with mastering your own thoughts, and watch how your influence grows—begin with your mindset and see how far it takes you.

As we close in on the conclusion of this chapter, I believe it is worth reemphasizing that the best shortcut to maximizing your leadership development, ability, and impact is to work your areas of strength. Remember, the work of life is to develop *your* gift.

No one has ever become a leader in their field by pursuing the wrong field. Why bother trying to improve in an area where you lack natural talent or gifting? You'll see a much higher return on investment (ROI) by focusing on developing your strengths, rather than improving your weaknesses, unless absolutely necessary or related to character flaws.

So, strive to be the best ________________ (fill in the blank) you can be by consistently working hard, learning, and continually improving. This dedication is key to achieving greatness, regardless of the field you pursue. It's how you become a leader.

Balance: Key to a Leader's Wholeness

Ever since I've been teaching, writing, and studying leadership, I have embraced and taught the importance of being or becoming a well-rounded individual.

For instance, while there are introverts and extroverts, there are also, as we have seen, ambiverts. An ambivert is someone who has learned to thrive in both realms. It is a person who can be happy reading a thought-provoking book alone at home, but also thrive when out with friends or in social interactions.

While there are two brain hemispheres, it is possible to develop some strengths in both hemispheres. Both brain hemispheres are not mutually exclusive. It is possible to be both logical and ordered and artistic and spontaneous. Again, balance is key.

Similarly, if you already possess a high IQ, it is possible to develop or improve further in the areas of EQ and SQ.

Also, of the nine multiple intelligences, you can have two, three, or even five that you score highly at. In fact, most people are not limited to only one of the nine.

The point is this: you shouldn't limit yourself because of the way you're wired. Sure, you have some predominant leanings and preferences as a result of your wiring. Nevertheless, you can still decide to stretch yourself and improve where it would be beneficial or necessary to your progress as a leader of your gift.

To that effect, I like the prescription that was given by Jim Rohn:

"Each of us has two distinct choices to make about what we will do with our lives. The first choice we can make is to be less than we have the capacity to be. To earn less. To have less. To read less and think less. To try less and discipline ourselves less. These are the choices that lead to an empty life. These are the choices that, once made, lead to a life of constant apprehension instead of a life of wondrous anticipation And the second choice? To do it all! To become all that we can possibly be. To read every book that we possibly can. To earn as much as we possibly can. To give and share as much as we possibly can. To strive and produce and accomplish as much as we possibly can."

Susan Cain, the author of *Quiet,* once shared her experience of being compelled to become a speaker to land herself a publishing deal. According to her testimony, it was actually her publisher (or agent, my memory is hazy) who asked her if she could "put herself out there" in order to promote and market the book. Pushing the boundaries of her comfort zone, she accepted the terms. While she candidly admitted to being terrified of learning the art of public speaking at first, she did it regardless.

I was often taught by my mentors that *what I am most afraid to do is probably the thing that I should most be doing*. I was also taught to "do it afraid".

The point is this: God has equipped you with certain strengths, predispositions, and leanings, sure. But do not let those hinder you from expanding your horizons, stretching out further, and challenging yourself. That's how leaders grow, achieve, and impact others.

CHAPTER 10

Celebrate Your Independence

"The individual has always had to struggle to keep from being overwhelmed by the tribe. To be your own man is hard business. If you try it, you will be lonely often, and sometimes frightened. But no price is too high to pay for the privilege of owning yourself."

~Rudyard Kipling

As you have seen throughout this book, the essence of impactful leadership is captured in the idea that true leaders aren't driven by a quest for titles, fame, of followers. They are driven by the idea of making a difference.

Author Cathy Quartner Bailey made a brilliant observation in her writing:

"Great leaders don't set out to be a leader... they set out to make a difference. It's never about the role—always the goal."

This perspective diverges from conventional views of leadership tied to positions and emphasizes a commitment to meaningful change.

According to this philosophy, leadership thrives on purpose-driven endeavors, extending well beyond the confines of formal titles, which are usually devoid of any profound or lasting worth. It manifests as a force propelled by a vision and an unwavering commitment to positive transformation. The true essence of leadership lies in the relentless pursuit of transformative goals, attracting like-minded individuals who share a passion for impactful change.

Historical exemplars like Moses, Abraham Lincoln and Mother Teresa embodied leadership rooted in higher purposes, where their actions spoke louder than titles. Their focus on goals, such as the thriving of their countrymen or the alleviation of suffering, exemplifies leadership that transcends formal positions.

Furthermore, this perspective underscores that leadership is a dynamic, continuous journey rather than a static destination. Leaders inspired by the goal navigate challenges with resilience, humility, and a willingness to adapt. It becomes a process of growth and learning rather than a static role.

In today's landscape, where leadership is often associated with authority, followership, and hierarchy, this perspective offers a refreshing paradigm shift. It invites individuals to reflect on their motivations, recognizing that leadership is not about climbing ladders but about contributing meaningfully to societal betterment.

In essence, true leaders understand that leadership is about the impact and positive change they bring to the world. It is a purposeful journey, meant to encourage individuals to contribute meaningfully to the world and leave a meaningful legacy.

The Rise of the Sigmas

In recent years, the alpha male has become a well-established concept in contemporary psychology. The terms *"alpha male"* and *"beta male"* originated from studies of social behavior in animals, particularly among wolves, where researchers observed a hierarchical structure within wolf packs. It's worth mentioning that female wolves can also be considered alpha or beta. Most likely, you remember this zoological lesson from high school, just like me.

When applied to humans, however, these terms are often used in colloquial language to describe certain personality traits or social behaviors. The general consensus of what alpha and beta males (and females) are like is summed up below:

Alpha:

- Traditionally associated with dominant and assertive characteristics.
- An alpha male (or female) is often seen as confident, competitive, and successful.

- May exhibit leadership qualities and be socially dominant.

Beta:

- Traditionally associated with more passive or reserved characteristics.
- A beta male (or female) is often seen as sensitive, cooperative, and less assertive.
- May be perceived as less dominant in social situations.

It is also interesting to note that *alpha* is the first letter of the Greek alphabet, and *beta* the second. In the context of the alpha and beta males and females, the use of these terms draws from the hierarchical structure observed in wolf packs, where individuals were classified as *alpha* (dominant-first) or *beta* (subordinate-second) based on social behavior. The terminology was then adopted and adapted to describe certain personality traits or social roles in human contexts.

In recent years, however, with constantly evolving social trends and settings, we have witnessed the recognition of a new breed of men and women: the sigma.

The word *"sigma"* is also of Greek origin. *Sigma* is the eighteenth letter of the Greek alphabet. In the context of social dynamics, the term *sigma* has been used to describe an individual who is perceived as independent, self-reliant, and not conforming to traditional societal hierarchies.

Similar to *alpha* and *beta*, the concept of a *sigma male* (or female) is often used in colloquial studies of human behavior.

Here are some general characteristics often associated with the idea of a sigma male or female:

1. **Independence:**
   - Sigma individuals are often seen as self-reliant and comfortable in their own company.
   - They may prefer autonomy and resist conforming to group dynamics.

2. **Introversion:**
   - Sigma types are sometimes associated with introverted tendencies.
   - They may value solitude and recharge through time spent alone.

3. **Non-Conformity:**
   - Sigma individuals are portrayed as less likely to conform to societal expectations or traditional roles.
   - They may reject or be indifferent to social hierarchies.

4. **Adaptability:**
   - A sigma person may be perceived as adaptable and able to navigate various social situations without being tied to a specific group or identity.

5. **Mystery and Elusiveness:**
   - The sigma archetype is sometimes associated with an air of mystery or elusiveness.

- They may be seen as difficult to categorize or predict.

According to *The Urban Dictionary* (https://www.urbandictionary.com), the definition of a sigma (male) is the following:

"A more internally-focused sibling to the alpha male. While the alpha male quantifies himself on his high position in the social hierarchy, a sigma male prefers to forego the social hierarchy and need for external validation altogether and pursue internal strength instead. Essentially a "loner" or a stray man, although sigma males may have a close circle of friends and loved ones with whom they share a deep connection. The sigma male is not socially inept but simply socially disinterested. Prefers solitary activities where he doesn't have to play social politics and can simply focus on himself. The sigma male accepts that he does not need power over others as the alpha male desires, but rather needs only power to control himself and preserve his own autonomy from others. Sigma males are often pragmatic but may be seen by others as aloof, paranoid, secretive or selfish."

To be honest, I didn't discover the concept of the sigma male personality type until I was already past midlife. It resonated with me on a profound level. It even reassured me. You see, embracing leadership as an introvert often results in the adoption of sigma-type personality traits.

The extroverted *alpha* enjoys being in the spotlight while leading and/or influencing people. He will even aim for higher positions in the corporate hierarchy, sometimes vying for it with determination.

The less-driven *beta* is more comfortable following the alphas and offering a supportive role, preferably away from the spotlight.

The *sigma*, however, doesn't fit into either of those roles. As such, if a sigma doesn't fully know himself (herself), it can be a confusing, or even a painful, place to be. It was for me early on, as I often felt lonely or ostracized. But for the sigma male or female who knows and likes himself (herself), it is incredibly liberating and empowering to learn of this personality type and its purported behavior. It's like the ugly duckling's moment of realization that he was actually a swan from the very beginning.

Moreover, as I delved into the distinguishing characteristics of Alphas, Betas, and Sigmas, I came to a realization. Without exploring other male personality types like Gamma, Delta, and Zeta here for brevity, it became clear that the main leadership model we've been taught for decades—through books, workshops, conferences, and courses—has been presented predominantly within the framework of the Alpha model.

In other words, many of today's corporate leaders, authors, speakers, leadership experts and gurus are themselves *alphas* who, not surprisingly, are teaching others how to become alphas. And, as we have seen, this model's problem lies in the need for significant influence and a strong follower base to be deemed successful. So, when you really think about it, quantifying and/or qualifying leadership in this manner doesn't make any sense.

And so, the spread of sigma males and females is a breath of fresh air amidst the stark extremes of today's leaders, influencers, and their followers. It brings an element of balance to the prejudices encountered in the age of influence. While this may be just a casual observation, I find that *sigmas* share similarities with the middle class, which is pretty much extinct by now, as they didn't fit into either the poor or the rich category. Likewise, *sigmas* do not fit in with either those who wish to lead people or those who wish to be led. They have their own rhythm and don't conform to societal expectations. Sigmas march to the beat of a different drummer.

Eagles and Pigeons

As a homeowner on Prince Edward Island, I am quite fortunate. Not only is it a beautiful place to live, but I happen to live in the countryside. In the summer, I get to enjoy the sight of gorgeous green grass hills, blue skies, and Canada's most beautiful beaches. Better yet, all year long, electing to live in the forest behind my house, are bald eagles. I never tire of watching them, whether perched atop the highest tree, chilling with their keen eye out for prey, or majestically soaring high in the skies just above my home. They are a sight to behold, and a wonderful reminder that, indeed, *"they who wait for the Lord shall renew their strength; they shall mount up with wings like eagles; they shall run and not be weary; they shall walk and not faint."* ~Isaiah 40:31, ESV

Things weren't always like that for me, though. You see, growing up, I lived in Montreal—in some of its nastiest neighborhoods. There were no eagles there. No. Instead, we had pigeons. And lots of them. My dad used to call them "flying rats", and would urge me to steer clear of them, believing they carried nasty bacteria and illnesses. I didn't argue.

And so, I always had contempt for pigeons. Some would say rightly so. Conversely, I have much admiration for the majestic eagle. These two birds couldn't be more different.

Let's consider some of those differences.

- Pigeons congregate in large groups, sometimes of 50 or more. Eagles soar high, majestically, effortlessly—and alone. As the saying goes, *"Pigeons flock together, eagles fly alone."*

- Pigeons poop all over everything in their surrounding, and then strut around like they own the place.

- Pigeons settle for crumbs. Eagles don't settle. Period.

- The pigeon emits a low cooing, guttural, and familiar sound. The eagle emits a piercing, alerting, and unique cry that is heard far away.

- Pigeons hide from storms. Eagles fly above them.

- Pigeons only look down from their perch, with their view obstructed by buildings erected by others. Eagles have piercing vision, far-reaching, almost limitless, and they can see far beyond what others can't.

- Pigeons stand for peace, love, safety, and innocence. Eagles stand for freedom, power, boldness, and victory.

- Pigeons are a dime a dozen. Eagles are rare.

Remember the saying, *"Birds of a feather flock together."* So, if you find yourself flying with pigeons, you're flying too low. Show me your crowd and I'll show you your future.

So, in a world full of pigeons, be an eagle, my friend. See farther, fly higher, *and don't be afraid to fly alone.* As you do, you might even realize that you like it.

Detach Further from the Herd: Do Hard Things

A quick online search using the terms, "Do Hard Things" will yield two bestselling books with that same title. A successful performance expert and coach, Steve Magness, wrote one in 2022. The other was written back in 2008 (and updated in 2016) by two teenagers who desired to challenge the youth of their generation to *do hard things* in a culture of low expectation. I am more familiar with the latter. I even bought a copy for my teenage son.

The life-changing lessons in both these books are similar: doing hard things helps us to develop profitable habits, endurance, perseverance, and to build a life of success and even significance. Because, guess what? Studying is hard. Starting a business is hard. Marriage is hard. Relationships are hard. Raising kids is hard. Making money is hard. Indeed, *most of life is hard*. And nothing better equips us to deal with a hard life and growing as leaders than doing hard things.

In fact, life is so hard that most people choose to forego going all in—or living life fully. Bertrand Russell, in his book *Proposed Road to Freedom*, rightly observed:

"The great majority of men and women, in ordinary times, pass through life without ever contemplating or criticizing, as a whole, either their own conditions or those of the world at large. They find themselves born into a certain place in society, and they accept what each day brings forth, without any effort of thought beyond what the immediate present requires. Almost as instinctively as the beasts of the field, they seek the satisfaction of the needs of the moment, without much forethought, and without considering that by sufficient effort the whole conditions of their lives could be changed."

Despite the difficulty of life, the spirit of leadership within a man or woman requires that we do hard things daily. And nothing will detach you more from the herd mentality than doing those hard things. To truly stand out, you must defy the mediocrity that pervades our culture.

So, what are those *hard things*, you ask? Well, they can be tackled through simple changes in habits, such as…

- Reading a personal growth book, when you'd prefer binging Netflix.

- Helping a friend paint his kitchen, when a relaxing Saturday sounds more enjoyable.

- Cooking a meal for your family, instead of ordering out.

- Cleaning the house, before going out for activities.

- Reading your Bible, when skipping your devotional would buy you more time.

- Disciplining your child, instead of putting up with behaviors you hate.

- Working out on the stepper, when staying in bed an extra half-hour sounds much more inviting.

- Willfully engaging in hard physical labor, just for the discipline of it.

Jonathan Edwards, the aforementioned renowned puritan preacher of the Great Awakening, advocated for the daily pursuit of *doing hard things*. His *70 Resolutions,* which he wrote as a youth, stand as a testament to his method of self-discipline. While Edwards' resolutions may not explicitly address the concept of doing specific hard things, the principles embedded in them, such as wholehearted effort, piety, self-reflection, and alignment with long-term goals, resonate with the benefits often associated with facing and overcoming the hard challenges of life. I urge you to find and read *Jonathan Edwards' 70 Resolutions* when you have the chance.

Doing hard things could also be tied to achieving bigger, more significant goals that we tend to put off out of fear; things like writing that book, going back to school, committing to that girl you love by marrying her, buying that house, or starting that business. Remember that often, the thing we most fear doing is the thing we most need to do.

Another thing to consider is that Scripture invites us to "sanctify ourselves" (Leviticus 20:7-8, Joshua 3:5 & Philippians 2:12-13). The word *sanctify* in Scripture means to "set apart as, or declare holy; to consecrate."

One thing is for sure, in a culture where people always try to find the easy way out, *doing hard things* does set you apart from the herd. It consecrates you to a higher ideal. It makes you stand out. And, judging by the way things are and where the herd is going, you can rest assured that's a good thing.

Do Hard Things Independently

In a Harvard Business Review article from January 2005, late renowned management expert Peter F. Drucker wrote:

"History's great achievers—a Napoléon, a da Vinci, a Mozart—have always managed themselves. That, in large measure, is what makes them great achievers. But they are rare exceptions, so unusual both in their talents and their accomplishments as to be considered outside the boundaries of ordinary human existence. Now, most of us, even those of us with modest endowments, will have to learn to manage ourselves. We will have to learn to develop ourselves. We will have to place ourselves where we can make the greatest contribution. And we will have to stay mentally alert and engaged during a 50-year working life."

Throughout this book, I have stressed the importance of *self-leadership*. The ability to get up in the morning and "Just Do It" is not as common as we would think. Manny struggle to put one foot in front of the other unless they have people encouraging and backing them up. The spirit of leadership doesn't wait for people's cheers to roll up its sleeves and get its hands dirty. It doesn't seek exterior motivation, but summons an inner one.

The etymology definition of the word "independence" yields some revealing information. Here it is:

independence (n.) 1630s, "fact of not depending on others or another, self-support and self-government;" see *independent* + *-ence*. An Old English word for it was *selfdom*, with *self* + *dom* "law." It is attested from 1670s as *"one who acts according to his own will."*

Likewise, the etymology of "autonomy" also offers some good tidbits:

autonomy (n.) "autonomous condition, power or right of self-government," 1620s, of states, from Greek *autonomia* "independence," abstract noun from *autonomos* "independent, living by one's own laws," from *autos* "self" (see auto-) + *nomos* "custom, law".

For the record, I was raised by my single mother during two separate periods of my life, from ages 7 to 9 and then from 14 onwards. As you can imagine, this presented some significant drawbacks as a developing man, especially in my teens. Nevertheless, there were things my mom taught me that were quite useful. One of those things was *how to be self-reliant —* *i.e. autonomous.* Due to her circumstances, my mother had to become self-reliant and develop a strong will. Consequently, she would frequently teach us the same things.

Although there is tremendous value in asking others for help, working with others, developing a powerful circle, and learning to be part of a team, I believe there is something to be said about the inner fortitude required to be successfully autonomous and independent.

Furthermore, there is extra significance attached to accomplishing difficult tasks independently. Sometimes, help just isn't available and there is no team around. Should this deter you from doing something productive, or even, God forbid, something hard? You've probably heard the old saying, "there is no "I" in team." But have you heard this version…

"There is no "I" in team. But there are two in "dedication" and three in "discipline".

Learning to tackle challenging tasks alone comes with numerous benefits. Firstly, it cultivates self-reliance and independence, which in turn catalyzes into discipline and resilience. It also hones problem-solving skills as you confront and overcome obstacles without external assistance. This experience builds confidence. It enhances your ability to face adversity in various aspects of life. Here is a list of the benefits fostered through doing hard things independently:

- **Self-Reliance:** Independence and the ability to rely on oneself in challenging situations.

- **Personal Growth:** A catalyst for individual development and a deeper understanding of one's capabilities.

- **Resilience:** Building emotional strength to bounce back from setbacks and adversity.

- **Problem-Solving Skills:** Enhancing the capacity to analyze, strategize, and overcome complex challenges.

- **Confidence Boost:** Successfully navigating difficult tasks alone instills a sense of accomplishment and self-assurance.

- **Adaptability:** Learning to adapt to changing circumstances and finding solutions independently.

- **Decision-Making:** Sharpening decision-making skills by taking sole responsibility for outcomes.

- **Resourcefulness:** Developing the ability to make the most of available resources and find creative solutions.

- **Empowerment:** Gaining a sense of empowerment through the mastery of difficult tasks without external assistance.

- **Autonomy:** Developing a sense of autonomy and the freedom to take ownership of one's journey.

- **Character Building:** Contributing to the formation of a resilient and well-rounded character.

Doing hard things is, in and of itself, a blessing—albeit often in disguise. In a world where we are often urged to do things through board meetings, teams, or committees, and where self-sufficiency is often viewed suspiciously, doing hard things alone sounds counter-productive, doesn't it? Some would probably (and rightly) argue that it takes more of your time and energy. But consider the differing point of view of these impactful leaders:

"A man can be himself only so long as he is alone; and if he does not love solitude, he will not love freedom; for it is only when he is alone that he is really free." ~Arthur Schopenhauer

"Work alone, not on a team, not on a committee." ~Steve Wozniak

"Without great solitude, no serious work is possible." ~Pablo Picasso

"The mind is sharper and keener in seclusion and uninterrupted solitude." ~Nikola Tesla

"Shakespeare, Leonardo da Vinci, Benjamin Franklin and Abraham Lincoln never saw a movie, heard a radio or looked at television. They had 'loneliness' and knew what to do with it. They were not afraid of being lonely because they knew that was when the creative mood in them would work." ~Carl Sandburg, poet, writer, and three-time Pulitzer Prize winner.

Do Hard Things Stoically

Over the past few years, I've observed a growing interest in stoicism among leaders and entrepreneurs. Popular secular podcasters ranging from Joe Rogan, to Tim Ferris, to Tom Bilyeu, have embraced it, discussed the topic, and/or interviewed guests who embrace this ancient philosophy. While stoicism lacks the redeeming presence of Christ, it offers a firm foundation of wisdom for many youths, both men and women alike. Considering where we find ourselves as a society, I find this surging interest in ancient wisdom refreshing—encouraging even.

Stoicism is a philosophical approach to life that originated in ancient Greece and Rome, founded on the belief that individuals can attain true happiness and fulfillment by cultivating virtues, exercising rationality, and accepting the inevitable challenges and uncertainties of the world with equanimity. The most highly regarded stoic philosophers are:

Zeno of Citium, Marcus Aurelius, Seneca, and Epictetus. Some of them are quoted in this book.

In many regards, I present here a stoic approach to leadership.

Central to Stoicism is the notion that one has control over their own thoughts, actions, and reactions, while external events are beyond their control. This philosophy encourages individuals to focus on what they can control, foster resilience in the face of what they can't, and embrace a sense of tranquility in the midst of life's inevitable ups and downs.

Stoicism thus provides a practical framework for moral living, emphasizing the development of the seven cardinal virtues, such as prudence, justice, temperance, courage, faith, hope, and charity. Ultimately, the Stoic mindset promotes a harmonious alignment with *natural law*, encouraging a resilient and purposeful way of navigating the complexities of life.

What I appreciate about Stoicism is that it instills a sense of purpose that transcends the need for immediate validation, allowing leaders to stay true to their mission and contribute meaningfully to their chosen endeavors, even in the absence of widespread recognition or a large following.

The spirit of leadership is essentially the living out of a stoic mindset. And while this can never replace the importance of faith in Christ, it nonetheless complements it. Of course, as in all things, God's truth provides the missing pieces of the puzzle.

In my own life, I unknowingly embraced the old-school thought-system of stoicism even before understanding its definition.

For the longest time, my writing and podcasting efforts went almost unacknowledged and definitely uncelebrated.

When I did a live teaching podcast/broadcast, streamed on YouTube and Facebook simultaneously, I had, on average, between one and three listeners per live episode. Not what you could call a smashing success. But I continued this way for over three years and 185 episodes. Every time I logged on to go live, I taught and preached as if there were 40,000 listeners. Every. Single. Time. For over three years. Likewise, I wrote every single book as if it were tied to a publishing deadline and contract, giving it my all.

Perhaps you could argue that, after three full years of podcasting, 12 books, and roughly 300 YouTube videos, I have gathered a respectable following. Okay, granted; I have more followers now than when I started out. Nevertheless, as far as *massive influence* is concerned, I'm still very much a work in progress. And you know what? The stoic in me is fine with that.

Do Hard Things Until

"How long should you try? Until. [...] Promise yourself you'll read the books until your skills change. You'll go to seminars until you get a handle on it. You'll listen to it until it makes sense. You'll go for it until you understand it. Never give up until—however long that is. Step by step, piece by piece, book by book." ~Jim Rohn

As you navigate your leadership journey, there will be moments of success and moments of failure—mountaintops and valleys. Neither of these two occurrences should be seen as final. They are not intended as a signal to stop. After all, the journey continues until He calls us home, right?

With that said, *the spirit of leadership* dictates that for every time you fail, or even when you succeed, you should take the time to pause, think, and reflect. This will assist in correcting blind spots, igniting new ideas, and reinvigorating yourself. When it comes down to it, leaders are constantly adapting, reassessing, and starting over. As Jim Rohn's quote above suggests, leaders do hard things *until*. And often, they adopt new hard things to do.

Furthermore, as you strive to do it *until*, you should also do it *regardless*. Do it *until* and *regardless*.

Genuine leaders persevere…

- Regardless of immediate results.
- Regardless of approval or applause.
- Regardless of who's watching or following.

You're likely familiar with the legendary determination of Thomas Edison while inventing the incandescent light bulb, attempting repeatedly *until*. Some say it took him 1,000 tries, others claim it was closer to 10,000. Regardless. He did it *until*. He did it regardless.

In recent years, especially since the pandemic lockdowns, personal growth and entrepreneurial teachings have focused on the importance of "pivoting" or "shifting". This concept is crucial for leaders, as it refers to the ability to adapt, change direction, or adjust your approach when faced with challenges, setbacks, or new opportunities.

So, no matter the assignment, the project, the new idea or venture, do it until… and then do it again.

Be So Good They Can't Ignore You

The above saying, *"Be so good they can't ignore you,"* is by comedian Steve Martin. It has been a motivational phrase in my life for many years now. It was the answer the celebrated actor gave to a simple question: *How do you explain your success?*

His brilliant off-the-cuff response has fueled pretty much all of my entrepreneurial, ministry, and writing endeavors since I've heard it. It motivated me to overcome setbacks, heartache, and rejection repeatedly.

Embracing this philosophy is what pushed me to become the best author I possibly could. And then, further pushing my own boundaries, I began publishing my own works through Amazon KDP, creating my own publishing brands in the process (*Thriving on Purpose* and *Wild Remnant Publishing*). I also worked hard at learning the ropes of book marketing. I then learned how to promote these books in different ways, especially on Amazon. But I wasn't done yet. I then went on to perfect my design skills and began successfully designing my own book covers in Canva. I also began offering other authors coaching services online to help them write and market their book.

The point is: I constantly pushed myself to improve my skill set, knowledge, and results. I developed my gift—and still do.

Now, maybe you're wondering, "Did it work?"

While this is a worthwhile question, I can't answer it just yet. You see, I'm still working on *becoming so good they can't ignore me*. I'm doing it *until* and *regardless*. Someday, God willing, I hope to tell you about my journey to success.

One thing is for sure, though; this never-say-die philosophy aligns well with biblical principles of diligence and perseverance.

Put Yourself Out There

Once you have made the decision to intentionally bear fruit, what comes next? Simply this: your steady growth in developing leadership.

Once you have found something worth doing by yourself and you slowly work it out, you are wilfully engaged on your own leadership journey.

As you do, here are some practical applications to be mindful of…

1. Stay intentional
2. Be Patient
3. Keep Growing
4. Keep leading yourself
5. Keep building
6. Keep adding value to people

7. Stay the course
8. Dig your ditches (2 Kings 3:16-19—prepare for the harvest, aka: God's blessings)
9. Keep the Faith
10. Repeat (Steps 1 through 9), until…

This, dear reader, is the repetitive process by which we make ourselves valuable to our fellow man, and to the world at large. It is the courageous and relentless pursuit of purposeful living. It is the way of *the spirit of leadership* within every man (and woman).

I love how Jordan Peterson expressed the idea of this growth process in his book, *12 Rules of Life: An Antidote to Chaos.*

"To stand up straight with your shoulders back is to accept the terrible responsibility of life, with eyes wide open. It means deciding to voluntarily transform the chaos of potential into the realities of habitable order. It means adopting the burden of self-conscious vulnerability, and accepting the end of the unconscious paradise of childhood, where finitude and mortality are only dimly comprehended. It means willingly undertaking the sacrifices necessary to generate a productive and meaningful reality. It means acting to please God, in the ancient language."

But, What If…?

Now, maybe you've been living this way already. Maybe you've been working these things through, day in and day out. You might even have done it for years. Maybe you still have little to show for it. Perhaps you're even asking at this point:

"But what if, despite all my efforts and dedication, I still don't make it? What if I do this for years and I end up like Van Gogh, Tesla, or Jeremiah—alone, disheartened, and unsuccessful?"

Dear friend, may it never be!

My wish for you is that you make yourself valuable, and that through wholeheartedly embracing *the spirit of leadership* so prevalent in this book, you add value to thousands upon thousands, millions upon millions, and end up successful and celebrated beyond your wildest dreams.

It is also my hope that you will not give up, ever. That if you fail, you will try again and again. That you will do it *until*.

With that said, however; if ever, God forbid, you do not succeed; always remember that your worth and value don't depend on how things are going.

Contrary to popular belief, having no followers or success to show for in no way diminishes your worth, your quasi-infinite potential, or your dignity. Failing doesn't make you a failure. Your value is inherent to your humanity, to your being made in the image of God. Therefore, your value is not subject to outside opinions, circumstances, or results. Ultimately, you carry the image of God, and the Kingdom of God is within you (Luke 17:21). That's what determines your worth.

Also remember that *"It is not what a man does that makes him great, but what he strives to achieve."* ~The Kolbrin, Book of Morals and precepts, 6:11

Indeed, there is often more glory in your pursuits than in the result attained by these pursuits.

We should all, therefore, adopt the simpler principles espoused in Ralph Waldo Emerson's poetic definition of success:

What Is Success

To laugh often and much;
To win the respect of intelligent people and
the affection of children;
To earn the approbation of honest critics and endure
the betrayal of false friends;
To appreciate beauty;
To find the best in others;
To give of one's self;
To leave the world a bit better, whether by a healthy child,
a garden patch, or a redeemed social condition;
To have played and laughed with enthusiasm and
sung with exultation;
To know even one life has breathed easier because you
have lived—
This is to have succeeded.

Failure Is Not an Option, But...

In my personal library at home, I have a funny little book whose title always amused me. It is called *Cheap Psychological Tricks: What to do when hard work, honesty, and perseverance fail*. By this title, the author, a psychologist no less, suggests that hard work and perseverance don't always work out for people.

That, dear reader, is a sad truth of life.

We've thoroughly examined this phenomenon throughout this book. The greatest efforts can sometimes yield little to no results. We've examined the numerous causes behind this disheartening reality, along with the various leaders who have experienced such an unfortunate outcome.

So, while ultimate failure is not an option, it is nonetheless a definite possibility. I am not saying this to be a lead balloon. I am only pointing to what is. To *reality*.

Nevertheless, a leader who adopts a stoic approach to this reality may find its inner workings rewarding and even worth it. I like the way John Ruskin put it. He wrote:

"The highest reward for a man's toil is not what he gets for it, but what he becomes by it."

Additionally, make no mistake; The Father, in His providence, desires for you and me to bloom into our best self—despite the odds and opposition of this fallen world.

I also believe that when people embrace their life's purpose, obey Him, and grow as leaders, it is not His will to see them fail. Call me naïve or idealistic, but I don't believe the Father wished to see Van Gogh or Tesla end the way they did. However, there is, as I have mentioned previously, another faction in this world—people who serve *another god*—the prince of this world. These *people of darkness* wish to stifle the light many of us carry. And their opposition often carries into limiting the level of success children of light can attain. I have been privy to many such testimonies throughout my life. These accounts can be disheartening.

The Plague of Elitism

One of the greatest quality a leader can develop is to face reality resolutely, without losing enthusiasm, and without trying to embellish it for the sake of accepting it at face value.

And our reality suggests that, as a leader in the western world, you will have to deal with the plague of *elitism*.

Wikipedia defines *elitism* this way:

Elitism is the belief or notion that individuals who form an elite—a select group of people perceived as having an intrinsic and desirable quality such as high intellect, wealth, education, power, physical attractiveness, notability, special skills, experience, lineage or other desirable traits—are more likely to be constructive to society as a whole, <u>and therefore deserve influence or authority greater than that of others.</u> And these people vouch for one another.

Indeed, look around.

Only a select minority rise to the top of their respective fields, despite the many who gave just as much blood, sweat, and tears to do so.

- Only a select minority of rivers have all the water.

- Only a select minority of countries have all the wealth.

- Only a select minority of athletes score the majority of the goals.

- Only a select minority of authors sell most of the books.

- Only a select minority of artists bask in the glory of renown.

- Only a select minority of individuals has all the wealth, esteem, and prestige.

Now, ask yourself…

Can you look at this worldly reality boldly and, despite its sting, keep moving forward with determination and confidence? If so, you will realize that the thrill is more often found in the journey than in the destination. You will also, most likely, find yourself persevering when most others faint or give up along the way.

Truth be told, there came a point into my author's journey when I found that my friend Roger Hataway was right. When, speaking of the publishing industry and his efforts to get his works published, he said, *"Elitist book publishing companies and their gatekeepers wouldn't consider it […]."*

Believe me, this is not just a fact limited to the publishing industry. It is an attitude prevalent across the board—in all industries. There are "gatekeepers" everywhere. There is, sadly, a strict hierarchical power structure of accepted knowledge, innovations, and technology in every lane, industry, and field. And when someone brilliant comes along with new, potentially disruptive ways or ideas that could threaten that power structure, they are usually denied entry by those gatekeepers. This, unfortunately, is the way of the world. And, yes, it is contrived. You don't believe it? Then just ask Nikola Tesla and some of the other leaders without followers who were discussed throughout this book. Clearly, many of them were denied entry.

So, as a result of this elitist mentality, sadly, some leaders succeed only after death, when their brilliance is finally recognized by others through...

Posthumous Success

The fact is that many of us yearn to achieve immortality, to be remembered after death, to leave a lasting impact. This desire, I believe, when rightly motivated, is stirred by the divine in man. Truth be told; however, we want posthumous recognition to begin while we're alive. Only those with the highest nobility of purpose consciously dedicate their energy to something that could be acknowledged perhaps only after their demise.

We are born without bringing anything into this world. Likewise, we die without taking anything with us. And the sad thing is that in the interval between life and death, most of us struggle over what we didn't bring and what we cannot take with us.

As you grow and mature as a leader, make sure you don't lose sight of the importance of sharing your gift and giving back—as much as you possibly can. And, as you do, never lose sight of where you came from and where you're going.

In addition, there are numerous blind spots in our current state of being here on earth. We often have no clue of the ripple effect of our benevolent actions and endeavors.

Surely, Van Gogh had no idea his works would be so prized one day. Nor did Jeremiah think he would be held in such high esteem as one of the greatest prophets of the Old Testament. Even the committed Nikola Tesla couldn't envision his now powerful legacy. But they accomplished their purpose notwithstanding. They dutifully planted the tree, and others sat in its shade.

There is a powerful song that was written by Ray Boltz in 1988, titled, *Thank You*. It tells the story of a man who, after having lived a life he thinks had little impact, ends up in heaven and is met by many individuals who walk up to him to thank him for the difference he made in their life. A segment of the lyrics reads like this:

> *One by one they came,*
> *As far as the eye could see*
> *Each one somehow touched*
> *By your generosity*
> *Little things that you had done, sacrifices made*
> *Unnoticed on the earth, heaven now proclaims*
> *And I know up in heaven*
> *That you're not supposed to cry*
> *But I was almost sure*
> *There were tears in your eyes*
> *As Jesus took your hand*
> *And you stood before the Lord*

And He said my child look around you
For great is your reward.

The Appeal of Your Uniqueness

"Uniqueness isn't a virtue, it's a responsibility." ~Mark Batterson

The reason uniqueness is not a virtue is because, at the end of the day, we're all unique. This doesn't consist of any special accomplishment. We were all born different in some way. Or, as a funny fridge magnet I saw read, *"Remember: you're unique, just like everybody else."*

Let's unpack this notion further...

My children love having birthdays. Consequently, they are always amazed at how detached I remain from my own birthday every year. One day, my daughter asked me why I don't care much about my own birthday. I told her, *"Because it doesn't depend on what I do in the course of a year. You see, no matter how good I am or not, or what I accomplish or not, I will see another birthday if I am still alive at this precise date next year. There is no special accomplishment in that. So, celebrating it seems somewhat pointless to me."*

Conversely, I give a lot more importance to my wedding anniversary. In my opinion, it is a much more significant milestone. It shows that someone made an effort. Indeed, intentional effort is required to make a marriage work—and to keep it going.

Although Elisabeth and I are not proponents of divorce, realistically speaking, one really bad year on my part as a husband could signify the end of my marriage. Heck, even one bad day or just one bad decision could do that! And the same can be said of her.

Similar reasoning finds its way in pastor Mark Batterson's quote: *"Uniqueness isn't a virtue, it's a responsibility."* Indeed, despite what our culture claims, uniqueness isn't a virtue. You're not special because you are different. You are special because of what you do with that difference. Therefore, in a very real sense, uniqueness is a responsibility; an important one at that.

Think about it. Only *you* can…

- Build what you will build.
- Create what you will create.
- Bring into existence your children.
- Sing the song that is inside you.
- Write the books that you carry within.
- Start the brand or business you will start.
- Bring to the world what you alone carry within.

All of these things, and many more, stem from owning up to the responsibility of your uniqueness. Embracing your uniqueness, therefore, means being responsible for it. It is through what you do that people will recognize your uniqueness. Even more, how you handle what you're given determines your leadership, regardless of whether others notice it or not. So, what we do or fail to do carries tremendous consequences. And it is only once we realize this that we take the responsibility seriously.

Doctor and missionary Albert Schweitzer, rightly observed:

"The tragedy of man's life is what dies inside of him while he lives."

Called to be Fruitful

In Scripture, Yahweh, our Creator, blessed Adam and Eve and told them to *"be fruitful and multiply."* (Genesis 1:28)

This, by the way, was not a mere suggestion. It was a divine call to purposeful action upon all of mankind. Notice how He first blessed them (empowered them), and then said to them (commanded them) to be fruitful. The call to be fruitful is, therefore, an intrinsic part of the human experience. As human beings, we are to bear fruit, whether spiritual, intellectual, or physical. Not only are we called to do so, but we are also wonderfully equipped (blessed) to do so.

Like our Creator, we too are tripartite (made of three parts). We have a body, a soul, and a spirit. In order to benefit mankind and bring glory to God, all three parts of our being must be engaged in our self-discovery and leadership journey.

As you endeavor to develop your personal leadership, you will notice how it is a creative process of sorts. As we grow and develop ourselves, we are involved in an enriching progression where our thoughts gradually become things; products, partnerships, businesses, art, and so on and so forth.

In the same way God breathed life into Adam, we too breathe life into what we invest ourselves in. That's the essence of human fruitfulness, as prompted by God. It all begins with a decision—an agreement with the Creator. This agreement is simple, yet profound. It says, *"Yes. I will obey You and I will be fruitful."*

Consider as an inspiration these wise words from a frail Catholic nun who worked in Calcutta, India:

"God has not called me to be successful; He has called me to be faithful." ~Mother Teresa

Make Your Light Shine

"You are the light of the world. [...] Let your light so shine before men, that they may see your good works and glorify your Father in heaven." ~Matthew 5:14 & 16, NKJV

Each of us carries a unique light bestowed by the Father of lights (James 1:17). The spirit of leadership, when we choose to embrace it, is what makes this light emanate from us and visible to all.

Some of us emit a gentle candlelight, while others radiate like a 40-watt bulb, a 60-watt glow, or a brilliant 100-watt luminosity. There are even those who emit radiance like bright neon lights. Other yet carry lights that provide guidance, some illuminating areas as vast as lighthouses, others offering a more concentrated beam, a precise dispelling of darkness, more like flashlights. Some lights even cut through steel, like lasers. The beauty lies in our both our uniqueness and our diversity, for we are not meant to radiate in uniformity, but rather to obey the command to let *our light* shine before men. This means your unique brightness.

And yet, despite this diversity in brightness, every light possesses a distinct purpose. Imagine a romantic dinner bathed in neon light rather than the warm glow of a candle. How would that fare? Conversely, would you navigate a warehouse in the dim light of a candle, or would you prefer the radiant brightness of neon lights? Much like the various wattages cater to specific needs, your unique radiance serves a purpose intricately linked to your individuality and the service you are meant to offer your fellow man.

In this grand tapestry of lights sent forth by the Father of lights, the key is not to be swayed by the radiance of others, but *to let your light shine brightly before men*. Make no mistake, your unique divinely tuned light is needed. It offers an inimitable radiance, a reflection of your purpose, an embodiment of who you are, an echo of the One who sent you, and only you can carry its finely tuned brilliance.

And so it is with your leadership, dear reader. It is unique. Make no mistake; It is needed. This can only be accomplished by you, in your current location and at this moment in history.

With renewed eyes, therefore, reflect on the enduring wisdom contained in the lyrics of this familiar nursery song that you may have sung as a child:

"This little light of mine, I'm gonna let it shine! […] I'm going to let it shine. Let it shine, all the time, let it shine. Hide it under a bushel? No! I'm going to let it shine!"

What Will Your Tombstone Epitaph Say?

The tongue-in-cheek and popular statement, *"Live in such a way that no one will have to lie at your funeral,"* serves as a powerful reminder of how we should aspire to conduct our lives. It underscores the importance of integrity, authenticity, diligence, kindness, industry, and the lasting impact of our actions and choices.

Ultimately, living in such a way that no one will have to lie at your funeral is about embodying the best God had in mind when he created humanity—despite our imperfection. It's about life lived with purpose, passion, and a deep sense of responsibility towards the imprint we are to leave behind. This approach to life not only enriches our own journey but also uplifts those around us.

The following text comprises a lesson penned by Charles Schulz, the creator of the 'Peanuts' comic strip. Schulz was a godly man who understood much about meaningful purpose and contribution. As you read it, you don't have to actually answer the questions. Just read it straight through, and you will understand where this is going.

1. Name the five wealthiest people in the world.

2. Name the last five Heisman Trophy winners.

3. Name the last five winners of the Miss Universe pageant.

4. Name ten people who have won the Nobel or Pulitzer Prize.

5. Name the last half dozen Academy Award winners for best actor and actress.

6. Name the last decade's worth of World Series winners.

So, how did you do?

The point is, none of us remember the headliners of yesterday.

And these are no second-rate achievers, either. They are the best in their fields—those whom we would consider *leaders*, *influencers*, men and women of renown.

But clearly, the applause dies. Awards tarnish. Achievements are forgotten. Accolades and certificates are buried with their owners.

So, here's another quiz. See how you do on this one:

1. List a few teachers who aided your journey through school.

2. Name three friends who have helped you through a difficult time.

3. Name five people who have taught you something worthwhile.

4. Think of a few people who have made you feel appreciated and special!

5. Think of five people you enjoy spending time with.

Was this easier?

The lesson is simple. The people who make a difference in your life are not the ones with the most credentials, the most money, or the most awards.

They simply are the ones who care the most. They were just there... *for you.*

Similarly, it is important to remember that our true influence lies in the simplest acts of service and care, regardless of our grandiose ideas and projects. This, too, embodies the spirit of leadership.

In the end, this is the epitaph people will remember when they stand before your tombstone: what you engraved upon their hearts through your steadfast leadersh...um, er, I mean, *service.*

Only Followers Where We're Headed

No matter how much we strive on earth to gather followers or to leave our mark, the truth is, there are no 'leaders' and 'followers' in the Kingdom of God—not in the traditional sense, anyway. Or, perhaps I should say, we will all be followers.

Indeed, each of us, when we cross over, will have our appraisal done by the King himself—The Lord Jesus Christ. He is the one who has all the following in the Kingdom. In the end, we will hear one of either two things, *"Well done good and faithful servant"* (Mat. 25:23), or the dreaded, *"I never knew you; depart from Me, you who practice lawlessness!"* (Mat. 7:23).

Notice how Christ, even through His praise, will *not* say to anyone, *"Well done good and faithful leader."* No. He will call us what we truly are... *servants.*

And, while some of us may gather a following on earth, we must never lose sight of how the Creator Himself has established leadership in the Kingdom. He said, *"But he that is greatest among you shall be your servant. And whosoever shall exalt himself shall be abased; and he that shall humble himself shall be exalted."* ~Matthew 23:11-12, NKJV

There's an interesting dichotomy that exists here, which is actually quite amusing. While there are no leaders in heaven, there are many who will receive honor nonetheless—*crowns*, the Bible says. And a crown, interestingly, is a mark of leadership or authority. So, in that sense, there is leadership recognition in the Kingdom. Likewise, while we will not have any followers per se, for everyone is a follower in the Kingdom. We all will unreservedly follow the King of kings and Lord of lords. In some strange way, in the Kingdom, everyone is a follower, but everyone is also a leader. We are all kings, but there is only one King of kings.

So then, these crowns, what will we do with them in the end? Simple. We will humbly lay them at his feet.

In my book *Kingdom Fundamentals*, I wrote the following, which is appropriate to share here:

"Citizens in the Kingdom of God are exhorted to serve and anointed to rule."

Declare Your Independence

It is only fitting, I believe, that as I bring this book to a close, the wisdom of Dr. Myles Munroe should again be brought to the forefront when he said:

"People who changed the world have declared independence from other people's expectations."

Throughout these pages, we have delved, time and again, into the importance of embracing your individual leadership and recognizing the responsibility that comes with being unique. The notion of breaking free from societal definitions, norms, and expectations aligns with our exploration of the vivacity of the spirit of leadership and the impact of your distinctive voice and contributions.

Just as those who have left an indelible mark on history declared their independence from conventional norms, so too should you find inspiration to chart your own course.

So, let the echo of Dr. Munroe's quote be a constant reminder, encouraging you to free yourself from these external expectations, and embrace the transformative power of being the leader you are meant to be—whether you're leading millions or, like me, perhaps only taking a walk.

Remember that ultimately it is through your *declaration of independence* from other people's expectation, and through embracing God's unique will and purpose for your life, that your true greatness will emerge, hopefully leaving an enduring legacy for the next generation, and the ones after that.

Poetic Justice

As you reach the end of this book, I wish to re-emphasize the importance for you to understand and appropriate the notion that *you do not need followers to be a leader.*

I believe I made this abundantly clear throughout.

Let me emphasize that I am not particularly skilled in poetry and never pretended to be. But, if you will humor me, I believe you'll appreciate this short non-rhyming poem, a blank verse I wrote about leadership—about the spirit of leadership.

I believe it offers a fitting conclusion for this work.

SHOW ME A MAN

Show me a man who leads his life instead of accepting it.

Show me a man who knows why he was born, who knows to number his days, and who knows how to live and die with honor.

Show me a man who is smart enough to know his flaws, humble enough to admit them, and brave enough to redress them.

Show me a man who cares not about honor, glory, or worldly titles, but about serving his fellow man to the best of his ability.

Show me a man who believes purpose is greater than riches, kindness is greater than popularity, and charity is greater than lofty dreams.

Show me a man whose vision includes imagination, a plan, others, and a legacy.

Show me a man willing to give away his last dime to help a stranger in need.

Show me a man who is acutely self-aware.

Show me a man who shares ideas instead of gossip or information.

Show me a man who is industrious, disciplined, and pious.

Show me such a man, and I care not if he was born in the city or in the country, in the slums or in a palace.

I care not if he has followers, success, riches, status, or influence…

I will show you a leader among men.

In the end, dear reader and leader, you must come to a place where you fully embrace that *it's not about you*, but about others. It's not just your life, but His lived out through you.

Indeed, if you can make it about others, without any expectations of them following you in return; that's the extent, beauty, and power of embracing *the spirit of leadership* in the age of influence and narcissism.

May God bless you abundantly as you follow the path He has carved out for you, without worrying about who is (or should be) behind you.

And when everything is said and done, always remember…

You Don't Need Followers to Be a Leader

APPENDIX I

More Thoughts for the Journey

Throughout my lengthy research and writing of this manuscript, I have discovered numerous valuable thoughts, poems, and prayers. While I shared many in the book, not all met certain criteria or were fitting for my thoughts as I wrote them down.

So, in this appendix, I provide you with some valuable extra material that will no doubt enhance your leadership journey.

DESIDERATA

Desiderata is a plural Latin noun, with the singular form *desideratum*, meaning *"things wanted or needed."*

Go placidly amid the noise and the haste, and remember what peace there may be in silence. As far as possible, without surrender, be on good terms with all persons.

Speak your truth quietly and clearly; and listen to others, even to the dull and the ignorant; they too have their story.

Avoid loud and aggressive persons; they are vexatious to the spirit. If you compare yourself with others, you may become vain or bitter, for always there will be greater and lesser persons than yourself.

Enjoy your achievements as well as your plans. Keep interested in your own career, however humble; it is a real possession in the changing fortunes of time.

Exercise caution in your business affairs, for the world is full of trickery. But let this not blind you to what virtue there is; many persons strive for high ideals, and everywhere life is full of heroism.

Be yourself. Especially do not feign affection. Neither be cynical about love; for in the face of all aridity and disenchantment, it is as perennial as the grass.

Take kindly the counsel of the years, gracefully surrendering the things of youth.

Nurture strength of spirit to shield you in sudden misfortune. But do not distress yourself with dark imaginings. Many fears are born of fatigue and loneliness.

Beyond a wholesome discipline, be gentle with yourself. You are a child of the universe no less than the trees and the stars; you have a right to be here.

And whether or not it is clear to you, no doubt the universe is unfolding as it should. Therefore be at peace with God, whatever you conceive Him to be. And whatever your labors and aspirations, in the noisy confusion of life, keep peace in your soul. With all its sham, drudgery and broken dreams, it is still a beautiful world. Be cheerful. Strive to be happy.

~Max Ehrmann, 1927

The Serenity Prayer

Dear God,

Grant me the serenity

To accept the things I cannot change,

The courage

To change the things I can,

And the wisdom

To know the difference.

AMEN

A Leadership Prayer

Dear Lord,

I am honored to be your servant.

But as a believer, I know I am also called to lead.

I desire to accomplish that which you have put me here to do.

For the challenging tasks that lay ahead, please, I ask that You…

- Enable me to clearly hear your voice.
- Propel me into my purpose.
- Ignite my vision.
- Equip me with boldness.
- Endow me with resilience.
- Stimulate my imagination.
- Give me a tender heart.
- Cover me with thick skin.

And I promise, O Lord, to not falter in my commitment; to You, to the vision you give me, and to those I serve along the way.

AMEN

Leadership Quotes:

"If God has called you, do not spend time looking over your shoulder to see who is following you." ~Corrie Ten Boom

"Don't be scared to walk alone, and don't be scared to like it." ~John Mayer

"The wisest men follow their own direction." ~Euripides

"By working hard, old man, I hope to make something good one day. I haven't yet, but I am pursuing it and fighting for it…" ~Vincent Van Gogh

"Your value does not decrease based on someone's inability to see your worth." ~Anonymous

"A man doesn't plant a tree for himself. He plants it for posterity." ~Alexander Smith

"First, say to yourself what you would be, and then do what you have to do." ~Epictetus

"A leader is best when people barely know he exists, when his work is done, his aim fulfilled, they will say: we did it ourselves." ~Lao Tzu (604 BC – 531 BC).

"Often truly authoritative leadership falls on someone who years earlier dedicated themselves to practice the discipline of seeking first the kingdom of God. Then, as that person matures, God confers a leadership role, and the Spirit of God goes to work through him." ~J. Oswald Sanders

APPENDIX II

You Don't Need Followers to Be a Leader

(The TEDx Talk)

I'm including the transcript of a talk I presented at a conference in Charlottetown in 2018. It took place during a non-sanctioned TEDx Talk event.

The text encapsulates much of the content of this book. It also includes some original content that is not found in the book. I think you will appreciate it. Also, if you are a speaker, teacher, or pastor, feel free to use its content in your own presentations, teachings, and talks.

You Don't Need Followers to Be a Leader

As we begin, I want you to repeat after me out loud: *"I was born to lead. This world desperately needs me and the unique gift I have to offer!"*

Okay, there is good news and bad news about what you guys just said out loud:

1. The good news: It is absolutely 100% true.

2. The bad news: Most of you, unfortunately, don't believe this statement.

But there's hope…

If I do my job well, you will believe it in the next 15 minutes or so.

So, here is my hope for this talk: I am hoping this talk I am about to deliver will deliver you.

I hope it will deliver you from:

- Low self-esteem
- False expectations
- Feeling like a failure
- Seeking approval
- And most of all… I hope it will deliver you from *seeking followers to feel validated.*

I have been on my leadership journey for years now. And when you study leadership you go to many conferences, buy a lot of books on the subject, and listen to a lot of *leadership experts.*

One of the main catchphrases in leadership development is:

"He who thinks he is leading, and has no one following, is only taking a walk."

Now, the first couple of times I heard this phrase, not only did I laugh, but I totally agreed with it. Why? Because it's true—right? Leaders lead people.

After I heard it a few times though, I've got to admit, I became self-conscious.

When this leadership proverb echoed in my head, I began looking over my shoulder. And lo-and-behold, for all intents and purposes, I had no followers to speak of. It seemed… I was only taking a walk.

I wasn't laughing anymore.

But, here is the thing: I began a deep introspective analysis of myself. Is it possible that I completely deluded myself into believing I am a leader? Did my reality check just bounce? Did I just pull the leadership equivalent of a bad audition on *America's Got Talent*?

You've all seen these, right? The person auditioning thinks they're 'all that', and they begin screeching for two minutes only to have the judges stop them mid-song and tell them: "That was absolutely ghastly!"

So, I did what any smart man would do in that situation… I asked my wife.

I went to her, and kind of sheepishly asked: "Dear… am I a good leader for you and our family?"

She said yes. Phew!!! Okay, so I passed the ultimate test — the wife test.

But I still wasn't able to explain my predicament.

Now, here is the truth: I wasn't a bad leader by any means.

I was just missing some vital leadership insight to understand *more specifically* what leadership is and what it isn't.

I needed to understand **the *spirit of leadership*** rather than **the fruit of leadership.**

In our culture we are taught that leadership is the distinct ability to lead people. That's it. That's the way I used to understand it. That's the way most people understand it as well.

But, there is a major problem with this philosophy. It focuses more on the results than the process. Think about it: How can you truly lead people you need? If you need followers to be a leader, your need of them should disqualify you from the mantle of leadership altogether. Followers need a leader, not the other way around.

So, I'm going to share with you guys the three leadership shockers that completely transformed my life and understanding of leadership.

Here comes leadership shocker number 1…

1. You are all called to lead.

You are definitely called to develop your leadership and to lead. Just not in the way we've been told.

The reason we cannot fathom that we are all called to lead is because we rationalize it this way: ***If everyone leads, who will follow?***

This dichotomy we have created in our philosophy between leader and follower is what prevents most of you from developing *the leader within you.*

We all possess leadership DNA because of what we are intrinsically as human beings.

The same way an acorn possesses the DNA of an oak, so are we all called to develop our own personal leadership.

So, you were born to lead, but you *must become* **a leader**. The same way the acorn was created to sprout and grow, **but it** *must become* **the oak tree**.

Here comes leadership shocker number 2…

2. You weren't all put on earth to lead people.

In our culture, developing your leadership is understood as becoming better at *leading people* and therefore becoming more influential and gathering more followers in the process.

Now you might say: "Sebastien, come on! That's what leaders do. They lead people and influence."

I'm not going to deny that. Of course, all of those who *lead people* and do it well are leaders. ***That's undeniable.***

Some of you were indeed ***called to lead people***. You are gifted in the areas of business management, or corporate, or social leadership. If that's the case, you are indeed ***called to lead people***…

BUT…

This is NOT the case for most of you.

You were not put on earth to lead people.

When I first realized this, it freed me from my own unrealistic expectations about myself.

When we believe that leadership strictly entails leading people, we mislead ourselves – pun intended.

Not having any followers doesn't mean you're not a leader.

Leadership doesn't require having 12, 12,000, or 12,000,000 followers—in fact, real leadership often begins with 0 followers, and a whole lot of people telling you that you're an idiot.

Why?

Because true leaders understand and apply leadership shocker number 3…

3. Each one of you is called to lead… in an area of giftedness.

You were put here to lead and to dominate in an area of giftedness. *You were put here to solve a problem. There is an assignment that only you can fulfill.*

The tragedy of life is that most people never discover what that area of giftedness is. And most of the time, they end up following those who have discovered theirs.

True leadership consists of self-discovery.

Here is a great definition of leadership:

True leadership is the discovery of what you were born to do and the willingness to do it no matter what.

Let me repeat that:

True leadership is the discovery of what you were born to do and the willingness to do it no matter what.

The truth is true leaders don't look back to see who's following. They don't care about that. ***They look ahead.*** They look forward to doing what they love and what they do best. They are obsessed with that. They want to be leaders in their area of giftedness… or what we call their field.

Okay, now that I've given you my three shockers, I need to expand by giving real life examples that will hopefully make all of this make sense.

Steve Jobs

Let's talk about Steve Jobs as an example. I have seen countless books, talks, and seminars where people talk about the leadership of Steve Jobs. They talk about him as a great leader—and he was. But was he a great leader at leading people? The answer is no. In fact, he was awful at it. Ask anyone who worked with him and for him: Steve Jobs had people skills, but they were all the wrong people skills.

However, Steve Jobs was a great leader in his area of giftedness, which was: ***innovation and entrepreneurship***. That was his area of gifting. He shared it with the world, and he dominated in it. As a result, he is considered a great leader.

Question: What was Steve Jobs concerned with? Having followers? Being liked? Or being the best at innovating in his field? The answer is obvious.

Vincent Van Gogh

Of his own admittance, Vincent Van Gogh was not gifted in leading or influencing people. He said, *"I do not say that my work is good, but it's the least bad that I can do. All the rest, relations with people, is very secondary, because I have no talent for that. I can't help it."*

He remained unknown most of his life, had no followers to speak of, and yet, Van Gogh is considered today *a leader in his field*, which was art.

So, was Van Gogh losing sleep over not having followers? No. Instead, he kept on painting… 902 canvasses, and over 2000 known works of art in all… in just 10 years. Even though he died unknown… he is recognized today as a leader in the field of art.

Wayne Gretzky

Wayne Gretzky is the all-time NHL *leader* in goals, assists, and points. He said, "You miss 100% of the shots you don't take." What do you think? Was Gretzky concerned daily with having more followers or with practicing his shot and passing accuracy?

Steve Jobs, Vincent Van Gogh, and number 99 were all leaders in their area of giftedness, whose only concern was to become better in their area of giftedness.

So, let's review the three leadership shockers:

1. As human beings, you are all called to lead.

2. You weren't all put on earth to lead people.

3. You are called to lead in your area of giftedness.

Furthermore,

Those who have developed a true spirit of leadership have these three distinct characteristics:

1. They have discovered their gift.

2. They are willing to do *whatever it takes* to share it with the world.

3. They don't care if anyone follows.

One of the greatest and most misunderstood principle in leadership goes against the grain.

It is the following: ***"Leadership means finding something worth doing by yourself."***

We often admire entrepreneurs in our culture. Often, we see entrepreneurs as leaders. As the movers and shakers of our world. Interestingly, the word entrepreneur comes from the French word: *Entreprendre. Entreprendre* means 'to begin something'.

When you begin something, no matter what that something is, you are alone most of the time. When you begin something that you believe in, you're often the only one who believes in it—you have no followers to speak of.

Now, I want you guys to repeat after me again what you said out loud at the beginning. And when you say it, I want you to think about everything you just heard here today. I want you guys to believe it.

All together now… Here goes…

"I was born to lead. This world desperately needs me and the unique gift I have to offer!"

Yes, it does. It really does. Believe it.

You might not have any followers in the beginning. You may even have people call you an idiot. You might even have a bunch of haters. But keep at it—no matter what. Eventually, to quote the movie *Field of Dreams*: **"If you build it, they will come."**

But even if they don't, it doesn't matter because you know what…

You don't need followers to be a leader.

ABOUT THE AUTHOR

Sebastien Richard is Montreal's own export to Prince Edward Island, Canada, where he lives the simple life—writing and publishing numerous impactful books, corralling three kids, and discussing Bigfoot sightings over pizza and movie nights. He's not just a solo act, though; along with his beloved wife, Elisabeth, he founded Thriving on Purpose Ministries (http://www.thrivingonpurpose.com/).

Born in the humbler quarters of Montreal to a family richer in love than money, Sebastien found his calling in the words of the Bible, His relationship with Jesus Christ, and amid the stories of the unsolved and the mystical. With his beloved wife, Elisabeth, his partner in both life and ministry, he embarked on a growth journey that includes publishing under his name and a not-so-secret pen name.

Sebastien's goal is to explore, inspire, and transform his readers, whether through dissecting ancient texts or researching new angles on leadership and faith. His books are more than just written words–they're a ticket to personal development, enlightenment, and a healthy dose of controversy. Sebastien is a bona fide Renaissance man, able to switch from ancient texts to modern conspiracies quicker than you can spell 'Renaissance'.

When he's not enjoying family time or serving up some biblical wisdom through his mighty pen, you can find him shouting at the TV during NHL games (go Avs go!) or chasing the truth about the latest fringe theory. Despite his love for the mysterious, one thing is abundantly clear: Sebastien's mission is to craft a legacy as impactful and intriguing as the faith and enigmas he cherishes.

MORE FROM SEBASTIEN RICHARD:

LEAD LIKE A SUPERHERO:

What Pop Culture Icons Can Teach Us About Impactful Leadership

Do you feel like there's more to you than meets the eye? Do you want to be inspired and empowered to become more and achieve more? More importantly... do you love superheroes?

Deep down, we all have a longing to be inspired and accomplish great things in life. Even as children, we often idolize our favorite superheroes. Their displays of power, strength, and bravery leave us in awe and serve as a source of inspiration. With the constant success of Marvel and DC Comic movies at the box office, these childhood role models often continue to influence us into adulthood.

Recognizing this phenomenon, leadership expert and author Sebastien Richard conceived a brilliant idea: to utilize these beloved characters as examples to encourage a new generation of leaders. This is how the inspiration for ***Lead Like a Superhero: What Pop Culture Icons Can Teach Us About Impactful Leadership*©** was born.

With a unique perspective on leadership, *Lead Like a Superhero* explores the strengths and weaknesses of today's most popular superheroes, such as Batman, Wonder Woman, Spider-Man, and Captain America, analyzing their leadership abilities. The book answers many profound leadership questions, linking them to fan-favorites, such as:

- What can we glean from the best leaders, such as Captain America and Optimus Prime?

- How could Batman plan more efficiently?

- What is the chief weakness of Superman as a leader?

- What about leaders with disabilities, such as Professor X, or Oracle? What do they bring to the table?

- What can be learned from those we dismiss as leaders, such as Wolverine or Spider-Man?

In total, the book features in-depth analyses of 12 well-known DC and Marvel superheroes, providing readers with a clear standard by which to evaluate leaders in their surroundings and inspiring them to develop their own leadership skills.

Lead Like a Superhero is a relevant and up-to-date resource, appealing to both comic book enthusiasts and individuals interested in personal growth and leadership. It is perfectly tailored for the next generation, serving as an ideal catalyst for their budding leadership potential through empowering values, lessons, and principles. It is the only book on the market that bridges the gap between pop culture and leadership, offering an unconventional, fiction-based approach to the pressing need for exceptional leaders.

Prepare to find yourself inspired, transformed, and empowered to *Ditch the Suit, Embrace the Cape* ©, and Lead Like a Superhero!

AVAILABLE ON:

amazon.com

KINGDOM FUNDAMENTALS:

What the Kingdom of God Means, and What it Means for You

How Much of The Kingdom of God Are YOU Experiencing? A Bit? Some? Not Enough?

Many believers lead lives of unavowed defeat, quiet desperation, and long for more in their lives and walk with God. The *victory, fire, living waters,* and *abundant life* they were promised, somehow elude them.

Has Christianity failed them? Has the Church dropped the ball? Is there something more? Something... *better?* The answer to all these questions is an emphatic *yes!*

The Kingdom of God was the central theme of Jesus' teachings. And yet, it has been (and still is) one of the most neglected and misunderstood teachings in Church history. Just as it was in Jesus' days, many are still bound by the *'doctrines and commandments of men'* today (Mark 7:7, Matthew 15:9). The results of this Kingdom neglect, which are found in most denominations today and in the lives of their congregants, are disquieting at best.

In ***Kingdom Fundamentals***, Sebastien Richard invites you to undertake and pursue your own *'Kingdom Quest'* by dropping the shackles of religion, redefining your purpose, and rediscovering the Kingdom God *'prepared for you since the creation of the world.'*

Within these pages, you will…

- **Gain a clear understanding of *God's mighty government,* and how it applies to your life here on earth**

- **Renew your understanding of *the Gospel and mission of Christ***

- **Marvel at the King of Heaven's *rules of engagement***

- **Understand *God's goodness and promises* in a whole new light**

- **Recognize *the crippling effects of a religious mindset***

- **Redefine and strengthen your *Kingdom identity***

- **Rethink your way towards *God's Kingdom abundance,* and much more!**

For God the Father, the Kingdom was meant to be our *immeasurable inheritance!* For Jesus, *His legendary legacy!* And for the Holy Spirit, *our dynamic destiny!*

The greatest issue with the Gospel of the Kingdom of God today is that believers think they already know and understand it. So, if you think you already know the *Kingdom of God* and its message, prepare yourself for a spiritual overhaul!

Encounter the glory of the Kingdom afresh through new and profound revelations of its King, its power, its majesty, and most of all, *your place and purpose in it!*

AVAILABLE ON:

amazon.com

ENJOYED THE BOOK?

If so, be kind and leave a review on: